more songs for Praise & Worship 7

MW00575074

PIANO / GUITAR / VOCAL EDITION

VERY IMPORTANT INFORMATION ABOUT YOUR CCLI LICENSE:
Possession of a CCLI license does not give you permission to make any copy of the music contained in this book. Even if songs are being used congregationally, the choral parts printed in this book may not be reproduced in any way using your CCLI license. If you are unsure as to what rights you do have to copy under a CCLI license or if you want information about CCLI, please call 1-800-234-2446.

COMPREHENSIVE PRODUCT LIST

	UPC#
CHOIR/WORSHIP TEAM EDITION *(Vocal Collection for the choir or worship team. Voicings range from unison and two-part to easy SATB. No accompaniment or chord symbols.)*	0 80689 51617 7
PIANO/GUITAR/VOCAL EDITION *(Spiral-bound book with piano arrangements containing melody in the right hand. Includes lyrics and chord symbols.)*	0 80689 32518 2
PDF File Library	0 80689 69587 2
Finale® File Library	0 80689 66187 7
Worship Planner Edition *(Spiral-bound book filled with worship planning resources to aid the worship leader, music director or pastor in planning and leading worship. Includes choir parts and chord symbols. No accompaniment. Includes devotional material for every song. Comprehensive indices for series on CD-ROM, affixed to inside back cover.)*	0 80689 65087 1

INSTRUMENTAL PARTS:

	PDF FORMAT	FINALE® FORMAT
Conductor's Score	0 80689 68487 6	0 80689 65887 7
Flute/Oboe/Melody	0 80689 68787 7	0 80689 66287 4
Bb Clarinet 1, 2/Melody	0 80689 67887 5	0 80689 65287 5
Bass Clarinet/Melody	0 80689 67787 8	0 80689 65187 8
Bb Soprano Sax/Melody	0 80689 67987 2	0 80689 65387 2
Eb Alto Sax 1, 2/Melody	0 80689 68587 3	0 80689 65987 4
Bb Tenor Sax/Baritone T.C./Melody	0 80689 68087 8	0 80689 65487 9
Eb Baritone Sax/Melody	0 80689 68687 0	0 80689 66087 0
French Horn 1, 2/Melody	0 80689 68887 4	0 80689 66387 1
Bb Trumpet 1, 2/Melody	0 80689 68187 5	0 80689 65587 6
Bb Trumpet 3/Melody	0 80689 68287 2	0 80689 65687 3
Trombone 1, 2/Melody	0 80689 69987 0	0 80689 67387 0
Trombone 3/Tuba/Melody	0 80689 70087 3	0 80689 67487 7
Violin 1, 2/Melody	0 80689 70287 7	0 80689 67687 1
Viola/Melody	0 80689 70187 0	0 80689 67587 4
Cello (Bassoon)/Melody	0 80689 68387 9	0 80689 65787 0
String Bass/Melody	0 80689 69787 6	0 80689 67187 6
Percussion 1, 2	0 80689 69687 9	0 80689 67087 9
String Reduction	0 80689 69887 3	0 80689 67287 3
Master Rhythm (single staff)/Bass Guitar	0 80689 69487 5	0 80689 66987 3
Keyboard/SATB	0 80689 69087 7	0 80689 66587 5
Lead Sheet/Chord Charts (C instruments)	0 80689 69187 4	0 80689 66687 2
Harp	0 80689 68987 1	0 80689 66487 8

For digital availability of these and other products, go to wordmusic.com

word MUSIC
& CHURCH RESOURCES
wordmusic.com

CONTENTS

ACKNOWLEDGMENTS

Word Music Committee:
Dale Mathews,
Publisher and Senior Executive

Sarah G. Huffman
Anissa Sanborn
Andrea Hathaway
Leslie E. Thompson
Ashley Miles Grisham

Senior Editorial Director:
Sarah G. Huffman

Project Manager:
David Shipps

Song Transcriptions:
Robert Adams
Lee Marcum
Paul Nelson
David Shipps
Luke Woodard

Piano Transcriptions:
Lee Marcum
Sandy Tipping
Luke Woodard

Vocal Arrangements:
David Wise

Orchestrators:
Robert Adams
Cliff Duren
Thomas Grassi
Michael Lawrence
Joel Mott
Tim Paul
Daniel Semsen
David Shipps

Editors:
Sarah G. Huffman
Anissa Sanborn

Bass Guitar Transcriptions:
Robert Adams

Guitar Fret Diagrams:
Lindsey Miller

Choir/Worship Team Edition Engraving:
Brent Roberts

Piano/Guitar/Vocal Book Engraving:
Ric Simenson

Instrumental Engraving:
Melanie Lawrence

Instrumental Editing:
Lee Marcum

Worship Planning Resources:
Devotions –
Marty Parks
Heidi Petak
Deborah Craig-Claar

Medleys – Marty Parks

Worship Introductions –
Cliff Duren
Kirk Kirkland

Production Layout:
Kim Sagmiller, Fudge Creative

Logo/Cover Design:
Dennis Hill & Kim Sagmiller

Copyright/Administration:
Sherrie Hensley
Joya Caryl

Production Assistants:
Anissa Sanborn
Robert Adams
Andrea Hathaway

Indices:
Anissa Sanborn
Ric Simenson

Alive

Words and Music by
ALEXANDER PAPPAS and AODHAN KING

VERSE 2, 4
Am C/E F F Am G
more than my words could say. I'll fol - low You, Lord, for all my days.
thing of this world will fade. I'm press - ing on till I see Your face.
13
Am C/E F
Fix my eyes, fol - low in Your ways, for - ev - er
I will live that Your will be done. I won't
16
F Am G
free in un - end - ing grace.
stop till Your King - dom come.
'Cause
f
19
PRE-CHORUS
Am C/E F F Am G
You are, You are, You are my free - dom. We lift You high - er,
21
Am C/E F
lift You high - er. Your love, Your love, Your love nev - er end - ing,
24

F Am G
ff
oh, oh, oh! You are a -
27
CHORUS
Am C/E F
live in us. Noth - ing can
29
F Am G
take Your place. You are
31
Am C/E F
all we need. Your love has
33
F Am G
set us free, oh!
35

INTERLUDE
Am C/E F F Am G
Am C/E F
Oh!
1. Repeat to VERSE 3
(to meas. 5)
2. to PRE-CHORUS
F Am G F Am G
mf
3. In the
Am C/E F
mp
Oh!
F Am G Am C/E F
mf
You are, You are, You are

F Am G
f
my free - dom. We lift You high - er. 'Cause
52
PRE-CHORUS
Am C/E F F Am G
You are, You are, You are my free - dom. We lift You high - er,
55
Am C/E F
lift You high - er. Your love, Your love, Your love nev - er end - ing,
58
F Am G
ff
oh, oh, oh. You are a -
61
CHORUS
Am C/E F
live in us. Noth - ing can
63

F Am G
take Your place. You are
65
Am C/E F
all we need. Your love has
67
1. Repeat CHORUS
F Am G
set us free.
(to meas. 63)
You are a -
70
2. SONG ENDING
F Am G
set us free, oh!
ENDING
N.C.
Oh!
73

Chords Used:

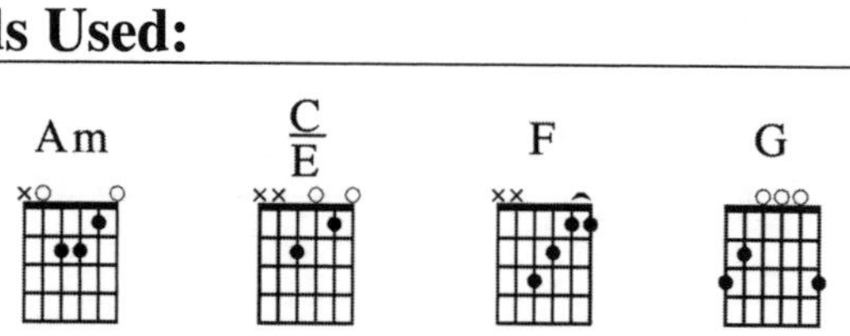
Am
C/E
F
G

All the People Said Amen

Words and Music by
MATT MAHER, PAUL MOAK, and TREVOR MORGAN

Am Em7 D
all you got to lean on, but, thank God, it's all you need.
13
CHORUS
G D G C G
And all the peo - ple said, "A - men." Whoa, and all the peo - ple said, "A -
15
D(4) C G B Em
men." Give thanks to the Lord, for His love nev - er ends.
18
C D C G C G
And all the peo - ple said, "A - men."
21
VERSE 2
C2 G D Em C2 G
2. If you're rich or poor; well, it don't mat - ter. Weak or strong,
23

D Em C2 G
love is what we're af - ter. We're all bro - ken, but we're
26
D Em Am Em7 D(4)
all in this to-geth - er. God knows we stum-ble and fall, and
28
Am Em7 D
He so loved the world He sent His Son to save us all.
31
CHORUS
G D G C G
f
And all the peo-ple said, "A-men." Whoa, and all the peo-ple said, "A-
33
D(4) C G B Em
men." Give thanks to the Lord, for His love nev-er ends.
36

1. Opt. Repeat CHORUS
(to meas. 33)
2. to BRIDGE
C D C G C G C D
And all the peo - ple said, "A - men." And all the peo-ple said, "A -
39
C G C G
BRIDGE
ff
C2 G D(4) G
men." Bless-ed are the poor in spir - it who are torn a - part. Bless-ed are
42
C2 G D(4) G C2 G
the per - se - cut - ed and the pure in heart. Bless-ed are the peo-ple hun-gry for an-
45
D(4) Em A D
oth - er start, for theirs is the King - dom, the King-dom of God.
48
CHORUS
G D G
mf–f
And all the peo - ple said, "A - men." Whoa,
51

C G D(4)
and all the peo - ple said, "A - men." Give
53
C G B Em
thanks to the Lord, for His love nev - er ends.
55
1. Repeat CHORUS
(to meas. 51)
2. SONG ENDING
C D C G C G
C D
And all the peo-ple said, "A - men."
And all the peo-ple said, "A -
57
Em C D C G C G
men."
And all the peo-ple said, "A - men."
60

Chords Used:

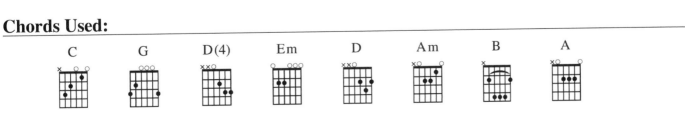

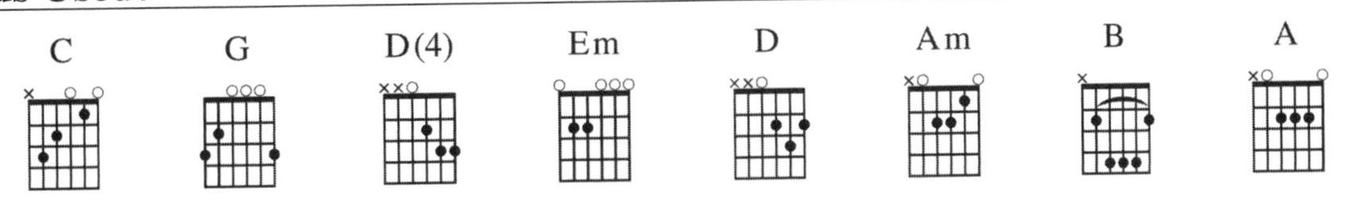
C
G
D(4)
Em
D
Am
B
A

332

At the Cross

Words and Music by
BENJI COWART, JENNA COWART,
MATT ARMSTRONG, and WILLIAM R. NEWELL

* *Alternate lyric:* **broken can be whole again**

D2
E/D
D2
mf
gain.
gain.
At the
9
CHORUS
A2
mf
cross
Your glo - ry bore my shame. At
11
Esus/G♯
the cross
You suf - fered in my place. You gave
13
1. Repeat to VERSE 2
D2
Esus
ev - 'ry - thing for us at the
15
(to meas. 3)
A
Bm7
Esus/G♯
A
cross.
17

2. CHORUS (cont.)
Esus
F♯m7
us at the cross. The
A2/C♯
Esus/G♯
Prince of Heav-en died at the cross, and
death became a lie. You gave ev - 'ry - thing for
D2
Esus
D2
us, ev - 'ry - thing for
Esus
BRIDGE
D
A
us. Mer - cy there was great and

F♯m E D A
grace was free. Par - don there was mul - ti -
29
F♯m E D A
plied to me. And there my bur - dened soul found
31
F♯m E A/D
lib - er - ty, at the cross, at
33
CHORUS
Esus A2
mf
the cross. At the cross Your
35
Esus/G♯
glo - ry bore my shame. At the cross You
37

D2
suf - fered in my place. You gave ev - 'ry - thing for
39
Esus
F♯m7
us at the cross. The
41
A2/C♯
Esus/G♯
Prince of Heav-en died at the cross, and
43
D2
death be-came a lie. You gave ev - 'ry - thing for
45
Esus
D2
us, ev - 'ry - thing for
47

Esus
mp
A
Bm7
us
at the cross.
49
Esus/G♯
A
A
Bm7
poco rit.
Esus/G♯
A
51

Chords Used:

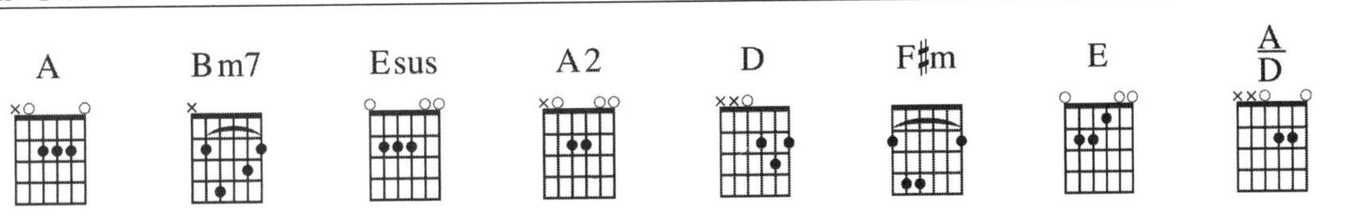
A
Bm7
Esus
A2
D
F♯m
E
A/D

333 At the Cross
(Love Ran Red)

Words and Music by
CHRIS TOMLIN, ED CASH, JONAS MYRIN,
MATT ARMSTRONG and MATT REDMAN

B♭ C/B♭ B♭2 C(4)
wide; where all the love I've ev - er
ness;
B♭2 C(4) B♭2
found comes like a flood, comes flow - ing down.
CHORUS
B♭2 F
At the cross, at the cross I sur - ren - der my life. I'm in
C Gm7 B♭2
awe of You. I'm in awe of You. Where Your love ran red and my
F C
1. Repeat to VERSE 2
Gm7
sin washed white, I owe all to You; I owe all to You, Je -

(to meas. 6)
B♭2 mp F B♭2/F F mf
- sus. 2. There's a
2. to BRIDGE
BRIDGE
Gm7 B♭2 Dm
all to You. Here my hope is found; here, on ho - ly ground,
F Csus/E B♭2
here I bow down. Here I bow down. Here, arms o - pen wide,
Dm F/C C ff
here You saved my life. Here I bow down. Here I bow. At the
CHORUS
B♭2 F C
cross, at the cross I sur - ren - der my life. I'm in awe of You. I'm in

Last time to Coda
(to meas. 67)
Gm7
B♭2
F
awe of You. Where Your love ran red and my sin washed white, I owe
42
1. Repeat CHORUS (as desired)
(to meas. 39)
2. to INSTRUMENTAL
C
Gm7
C
all to You; I owe all to You. At the all to You. I owe
45
Gm7
C
Gm7
all to You; I owe all to You. I owe all to You, Je -
48
INSTRUMENTAL
mp
B♭2/F
F
B♭2/F
F
- sus. Je - sus.
51
BRIDGE
B♭2
mp–mf–f
Dm
F
Here my hope is found; here, on ho - ly ground, here I bow down.
(play cued notes on repeats)
55

Csus/E
B♭2
Dm
Here I bow down. Here, arms o - pen wide, here You saved my life.
58
1. Repeat BRIDGE (as desired)
(to meas. 55)
2. to CHORUS
F
Csus/E
F/C
Here I bow down. Here I bow down. Here I bow down.
61
D.S. al Coda
(to meas. 39)
C
mf
Here I bow. At the
64
CODA
ENDING
C
Gm7
B♭2
all to You; I owe all to You, Je - sus.
67
F
B♭2
poco rit. to end
F
70

Chords Used:

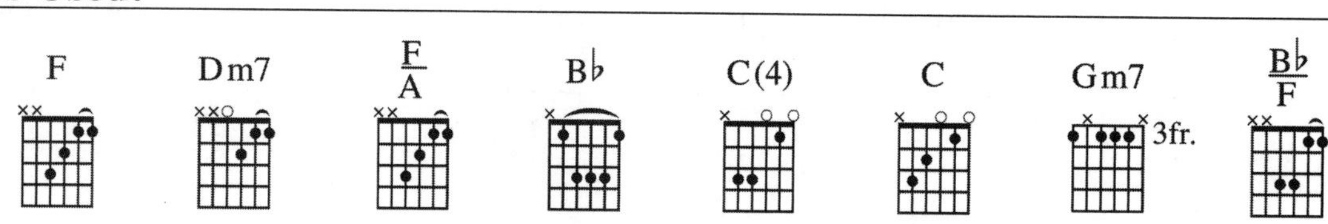
F
Dm7
F/A
B♭
C(4)
C
Gm7
3fr.
B♭/F

At Your Name
(Yahweh, Yahweh)

334

Words and Music by
PHIL WICKHAM and TIM HUGHES

Rock groove (♩ = 84)
G
Gsus
G
Gsus
Cmaj7
mp
VERSE 1, 2
G
mp–mf
1. At Your Name the mountains shake and crumble.
2. (At Your Name) the morning breaks in glory.
Cmaj7
G
At Your Name
At Your Name
Cmaj7
mf
the oceans roar and tumble.
creation sings Your story.
At Your Name

PRE-CHORUS
D Em C
mf
angels will bow, the earth will rejoice, Your people cry out.
13
CHORUS
D Gsus G
f
Lord of all the earth, we shout Your Name, shout Your Name,
16
C/E Em D
filling up the skies with endless praise, endless praise. Yahweh, Yahweh, we
19
1. Repeat to VERSE 2
(to meas. 5)
C2 Gsus G
mf
love to shout Your Name, O Lord!
2. At Your Name
22
2. to BRIDGE
BRIDGE
Gsus G D
mp–mf
There is no one like our God. We will
(2nd time play cued notes)
25

1. Repeat BRIDGE (to meas. 27)
Em C D G
mf
praise You, praise You. There's no one like our God. We will sing! We will sing! There is
28
2.
G
BRIDGE
D
f
sing! We will sing! There is no one like our God. We will
31
Em C D
praise You, praise You. Je - sus, You are God. We will
33
CHORUS
C D C/E D/F♯ D Gsus G
f
sing! Lord of all the earth, we
35
C/E Em
shout Your Name, shout Your Name, fill - ing up the skies with end - less praise, end - less praise.
38

1. Repeat CHORUS
(to meas. 37)
2. to SONG ENDING
D
C2
D
Yah-weh, Yah-weh, we love to shout Your Name!
Yah-weh, Yah-weh, we
41
ENDING
C2
Gsus
G
love to shout Your Name, O Lord!
44
C/E
Em
46
D
C2
G
Yah-weh, Yah-weh, we love to shout Your Name, O Lord!
49

Chords Used:

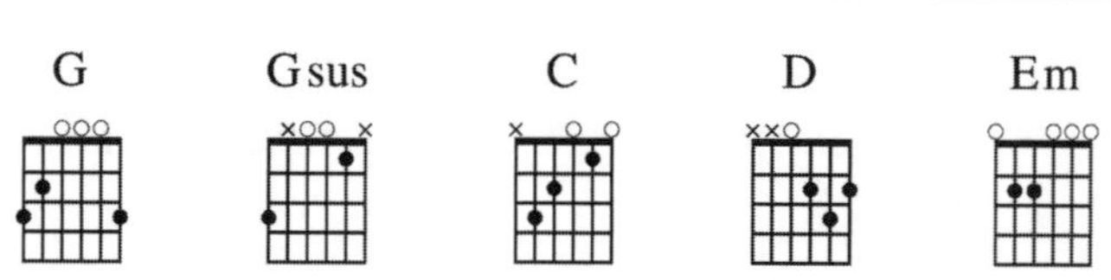
G
Gsus
C
D
Em

Break Every Chain

Words and Music by
WILL REAGAN

2. to INSTRUMENTAL
F♯m Dmaj7 A E/G♯
chain, break ev - 'ry chain, break ev - 'ry chain; to break ev - 'ry
F♯m D2 A E(4)
chain, break ev - 'ry chain, break ev - 'ry chain.
INSTRUMENTAL
F♯m A/D A E(4) F♯m A/D A E/G♯
mp
All -
VERSE
F♯m D2 A E F♯m D2
- suf - fi - cient sac - ri - fice, so free - ly giv - en; such
A E/G♯ F♯m D2 A E
a price bought our re - demp - tion. Heav - en's gates swing wide.

D.S. al Coda
(to meas. 5)
F♯m D2 A E/G♯
mf
There is pow -
27
CODA
A E F♯m D2
f
- sus to break ev - 'ry chain, break ev - 'ry chain, break ev - 'ry
29
A E/G♯ F♯m D2
chain; to break ev - 'ry chain, break ev - 'ry chain, break ev - 'ry
31
INSTRUMENTAL
A E ff F♯m D2
(1st time)
chain.
33
A E F♯m D2
(opt. Worship Leader ad libs)
1. Repeat as desired (to meas. 34)
A E/G♯
35

2. to BRIDGE
A E/G♯ F♯m D2 A E
mp
There's an ar -
BRIDGE
F♯m D2 A E F♯m D2
(2nd time omit ties in accompaniment)
- my ris - ing up. There's an ar - my ris - ing up.
1. Repeat BRIDGE
A E F♯m D2 A E
There's an ar - my ris - ing up to break ev-'ry
(to meas. 41)
F♯m D2 A E
chain, break ev - 'ry chain, break ev - 'ry chain. There's an ar -
2.
A E F♯m D2
f
to break ev - 'ry chain, break ev - 'ry chain, break ev - 'ry
38
41
44
47
49

A E F♯m D2
chain; to break ev - 'ry chain, break ev - 'ry chain, break ev - 'ry
51
INSTRUMENTAL
A E F♯m D2 A E
f
chain.
53
F♯m D2
1. Repeat (to meas. 54)
A E
2. to CHORUS
A E F♯m D2
mp
56
CHORUS
A E F♯m D2
mp–mf
There is pow - er in the Name of Je -
60
A E F♯m D2
- sus. There is pow - er in the Name of Je -
62

A E F#m D2
- sus. There is pow - er in the Name of Je -
64
1. Repeat CHORUS
A E F#m D2
- sus to break ev - 'ry chain, break ev - 'ry chain, break ev - 'ry
66
(to meas. 61)
2. to FINAL CHORUS
A E mf F#m D2
chain. There is pow - chain, break ev - 'ry chain, break ev - 'ry
68
A E F#m D2
chain; to break ev - 'ry chain, break ev - 'ry chain, break ev - 'ry
70
A E F#m D2
chain. To break ev - 'ry chain, break ev - 'ry chain, break ev - 'ry
72

A E F♯m D2
chain; to break ev - 'ry chain, break ev - 'ry chain, break ev - 'ry
74
FINAL CHORUS
A E f F♯m D2
chain. There is pow - er in the Name of Je -
76
A E F♯m D2
- sus. There is pow - er in the Name of Je -
78
A E F♯m D2
- sus. There is pow - er in the Name of Je -
80
1. Repeat FINAL CHORUS
A E ff F♯m D2
- sus to break ev - 'ry chain, break ev - 'ry chain, break ev - 'ry
82

A E F♯m D2
chain; to break ev - 'ry chain, break ev - 'ry chain, break ev - 'ry
84
A E
(to meas. 77)
2. SONG ENDING
A E
chain. There is pow - - sus to break ev - 'ry
86
F♯m D2 A E
chain, break ev - 'ry chain, break ev - 'ry chain; to break ev - 'ry
88
F♯m D2 A E F♯m
chain, break ev - 'ry chain, break ev - 'ry chain!
90

Chords Used:

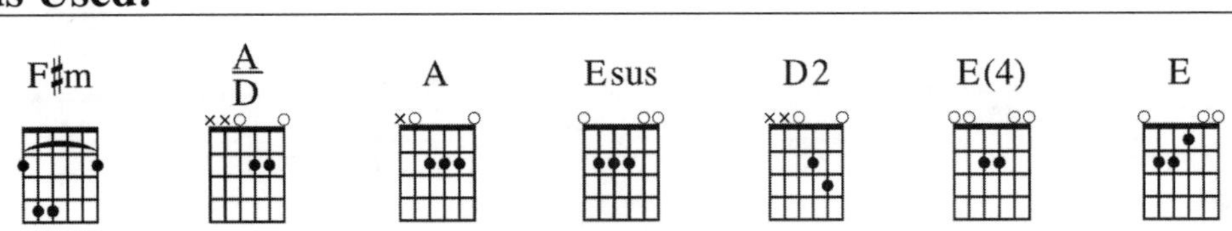
F♯m
A/D
A
Esus
D2
E(4)
E

Build Your Kingdom Here

Words and Music by
REND COLLECTIVE

Bright, folk feel (♩ = 134)

D D/F♯ G A D
ver - y souls. Ho - ly Spir - it, come, in - vade us
poor, at peace. We lay down our lives for Heav - en's
seed in us. Fill us with the strength and love of
A(4) G D A(4)
now. We are Your church.
cause. We are Your church.
Christ. We are Your church.
1. Repeat to VERSE 2
(to meas. 1)
G D A(4) D Dsus
We need Your pow'r in us. 2. We
We pray, re - vive this
We are the hope on
2., 3. to CHORUS
CHORUS
D Dsus A Bm
f
earth. Build Your King - dom here. Let the
earth.
G D A
dark - ness fear. Show Your might - y
12
15
19
23
27

Bm G A D A
hand. Heal our streets and land. Set Your church on
30
Bm G D A
fire. Win this na - tion back. Change the at - mos -
34
1. Repeat to VERSE 3
Bm G A D Dsus
phere. Build Your King - dom here, we pray.
38
(to meas. 1)
2. INSTRUMENTAL
D Dsus D Dsus D
mf
D Asus
3. Un - pray.
42
D Asus Bm A Bm A/C♯ D Asus
46

D Asus Bm A Bm A/C♯ D A/C♯
50
D Bm/F♯ G A/G G A Bm A
54
Bm A/C♯ D Dsus D D/A D
58
CHORUS
D6 A Bm G
mf
Build Your King - dom here. Let the dark - ness
62
D A Bm G
fear. Show Your might - y hand. Heal our streets and
66

A D A Bm
f
land. Set Your church on fire. Win this
70
G D A
na - tion back. Change the at - mos -
73
Bm G A
phere. Build Your King - dom here, we
76
D Dsus/A D Dsus/A D Dsus/A D
pray.
79

Chords Used:

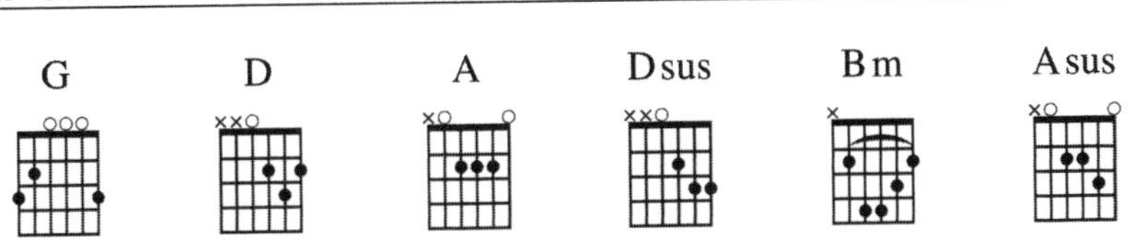
G
D
A
Dsus
Bm
Asus

337 Calvary

Words and Music by
JONAS MYRIN and REUBEN MORGAN

CHORUS
G
mf
Em7
C2
Cal - va - ry cov - ers it all. My sin and shame don't
11
Am7
G
count an - y - more. All praise to the One who has
14
Em7
C
D
G
ran - somed my soul! Cal - va - ry cov - ers it all.
2. No pow - er
16
VERSE 2
G
Em7
C2
on earth, not e - ven the grave, can sep - a - rate us from mer - cy
19
D
Em7
D/F♯
and grace. He is faith - ful to save; oh, His blood nev -
22

G C D G
- er fails. Cal - va - ry cov - ers it all.
24
CHORUS
G Em7 C2
f
Cal - va - ry cov - ers it all. My sin and shame don't
27
Am7 G
count an - y - more. All praise to the One who has
30
Em7 C D G
ran - somed my soul! Cal - va - ry cov - ers it all.
32
BRIDGE
Em7 C D
No one but Je -
35

Em7 C D
- sus could make us pure as snow.
38
Em7 D/F♯ G C D
We stand in Your free - dom. Cal - va - ry cov - ers it
41
CHORUS
G G Em7
mp–f
all. Cal - va - ry cov - ers it all. My
44
C2 Am7
mf
sin and shame don't count an - y - more. All
47
G Em7
praise to the One who has ran - somed my soul!
49

1. Repeat CHORUS
(to meas. 45)
C D G
Cal - va - ry cov - ers it all.
51
2. to TAG
TAG
C D G G
Cal - va - ry cov - ers it all.
All praise to the One who has
53
Em7
1. Repeat TAG (as desired)
C D
ran - somed my soul!
Cal - va - ry cov - ers it all.
56
(to meas. 55)
2. SONG ENDING
G C D G
rit.
All Cal - va - ry cov - ers it all.
58

Chords Used:

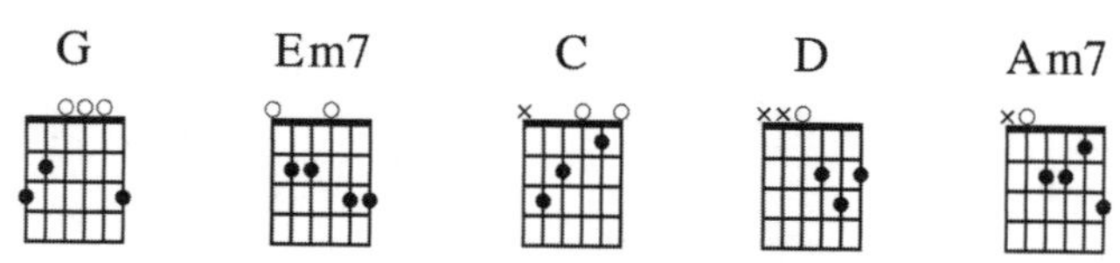
G
Em7
C
D
Am7

Christ Is Enough

Words and Music by
JONAS MYRIN and REUBEN MORGAN

Driving pop groove (♩ = 80)
Gm7
E♭2
mf
B♭
Fsus
A
Gm7
3
E♭2
B♭
Fsus
A
6
VERSE 1
Gm7
mf
E♭2
1. Christ is my re - ward, and all of my de - vo -
9

B♭
F/A
Gm7
-tion. Now there's noth - ing in this world
11
E♭2
B♭
that could ev - er sat - is - fy.
14
F/A
Dm
E♭
F
Through ev - 'ry trial, my soul will sing:
16
Gm
Dm
E♭
Gm
F
"No turn - ing back; I've been set free!"
18
CHORUS
B♭
mf-f
Gm
Christ is e - nough for me. Christ is e -
(2nd time play cued notes)
21

F
E♭2
F
Gm
nough for me.
Ev - 'ry-thing I need is in You,
24
2nd time to Coda
(to meas. 41)
VERSE 2
E♭2
F
Gm7
ev - 'ry-thing I need.
2. Christ, my all in all,
27
E♭2
B♭
the joy of my sal - va - tion.
30
F
A
Gm7
And this hope will nev - er fail;
32
E♭2
B♭
Heav-en is our home.
34

F/A
Dm
E♭
F
Through ev - 'ry storm my soul will sing:
36
Gm
Dm
E♭
Gm
F
D.S. al Coda
(to meas. 21)
"Je - sus is here; to God be the glo - ry!"
38
CODA
B♭
B♭sus
B♭2
mf
41
BRIDGE 1
B♭
mf
B♭
B♭sus
B♭2
B♭
I have de - cid - ed to fol - low Je - sus; no turn-ing
44
1. Repeat BRIDGE 1
(to meas. 45)
2. to BRIDGE 2
E♭
Gm
Fsus
E♭
F
back, no turn - ing back. I have de - back, no turn - ing
47

BRIDGE 2
B♭
Gm7
E♭
back. The cross be - fore me, the world be -
50
Fsus
B♭
1. Repeat BRIDGE 2
E♭
Gm7
hind me; no turn - ing back, no turn - ing
52
(to meas. 51)
2. to CHORUS
Fsus
E♭
F
back. The cross be - back, no turn - ing
54
B♭
B♭sus
back.
56
CHORUS
B♭
Gm
Christ is e - nough for me. Christ is e -
58

F
E♭2
nough for me. Ev - 'ry-thing I
61
F
Gm
1. Repeat CHORUS
E♭2
need is in You, ev - 'ry-thing I
63
F
(to meas. 58)
2. to BRIDGE
E♭2
need. ev - 'ry-thing I
65
BRIDGE 3
F
Gm7
E♭
need. I have de - cid - ed to fol - low
67
Fsus
Gm7
1. Repeat BRIDGE 3
E♭
Gm7
Je - sus; no turn - ing back, no turn - ing
69

(to meas. 68)
2. to ENDING
Fsus
Eb
F
back. I have de - back, no turn - ing
71
ENDING
Bb
Bb
Bbsus
back. I have de - cid - ed to fol - low
73
1. Repeat ENDING
Bb2
Bb
Eb
Gm7
Je - sus; no turn - ing back, no turn - ing
75
(to meas. 74)
2. SONG ENDING
F
Eb
F
Bb
rit.
back. I have de - back, no turn - ing back.
77

Chords Used:

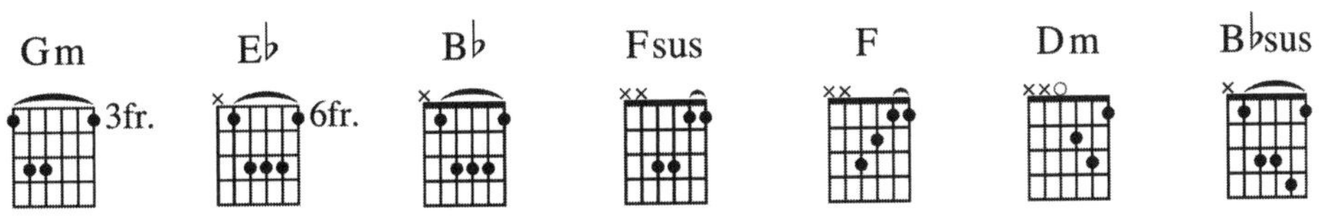
Gm
3fr.
Eb
6fr.
Bb
Fsus
F
Dm
Bbsus

339

Crown Him
(Majesty)

Words and Music by
CHRIS TOMLIN, ED CASH,
GEORGE JOB ELVEY, GODFREY THRING,
MATT MAHER, and MATTHEW BRIDGES

Reverently (♩ = 75)
Gm Eb Bb/D Fsus F
mp
VERSE 1, 2
Gm Eb2 Bb/D
mp
1. Crown Him with man - y crowns, the Lamb up - on His
2. Crown Him the Lord of life! Who tri - umphed o'er the
5
Fsus Gm Gm/F C/E F
throne. Hark! How the heav'n - ly an - them drowns all
grave, and rose vic - to - rious in the strife for
8
F/C C Fsus Bb2/D
mu - sic but its own! A - wake, my soul, and
those He came to save. His glo - ries now we
11

E♭2 C Fsus F
sing of Him Who died for me, and
sing, Who died and rose on high, Who
14
Gm Gm2/F E♭ B♭/D Cm7 F7sus
hail Him as thy match - less King through all e - ter - ni -
died e - ter - nal life to bring and lives that death may
17
B♭
ty.
die.
20
CHORUS
E♭2(♯4) E♭
mf
Maj - es - ty!
B♭maj7/D B♭/D E♭2(♯4) E♭ Gm(add2) Fsus
Lord of all! Let ev - 'ry throne be - fore Him fall! The
23
E♭2(♯4) E♭ B♭maj7/D B♭/D Cm7 B♭/D
King of kings O come a - dore, our God Who reigns for -
26

1. Repeat to VERSE 2
(to meas. 5)
Fsus
B♭
ev - er - more!
29
2. to BRIDGE
Fsus
B♭
f
ev - er - more! For - ev - er - more! All
32
BRIDGE
E♭
B♭/D
Fsus
hail Re - deem - er, hail, for
35
B♭
B♭/D
E♭2
B♭
He has died for me! His praise and glo - ry
37
1. Repeat BRIDGE
(to meas. 35)
Gm
F
E♭
Fsus
B♭
shall not fail through - out e - ter - ni - ty! All
40

2. to CHORUS
CHORUS
Eb Fsus Gm F/A Eb2(#4) Eb
mp
out e - ter - ni - ty! Maj - es - ty!
43
Bb/D Eb2(#4) Eb Gm Fsus
Lord of all! Let ev - 'ry throne be - fore Him fall! The
46
Eb2(#4) Eb Bb/D Cm7 Bb/D
King of kings O come a - dore, our God Who reigns for -
49
CHORUS
Fsus Bb F2(#4) F
ff
ev - er - more! Maj - es - ty!
52
C/E F2(#4) F Am Gsus C/E
Lord of all! Let ev - 'ry throne be - fore Him fall! The
55

F2(♯4) F C/E
King of kings O come a - dore, our
58
Dm7 C/E Gsus C
God Who reigns for - ev - er-more! Praise
60
TAG
Dm7 C/E Gsus C
God Who reigns for - ev - er-more! You're the
62
Dm7 C/E Gsus C
molto rit.
God Who reigns for - ev - er - more!
64

Chords Used:

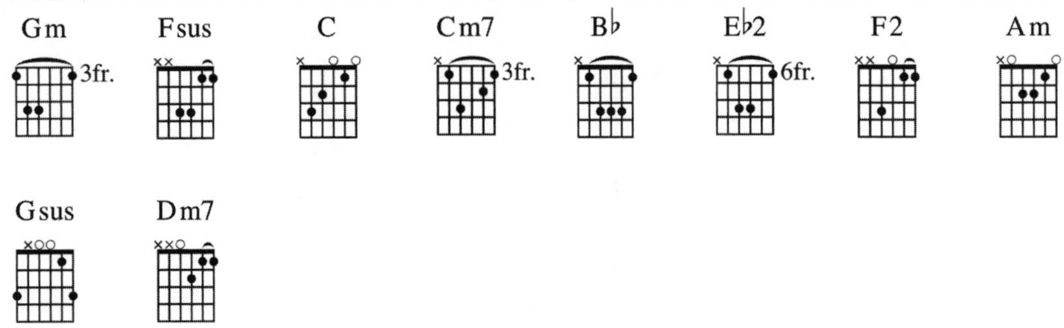
Gm
3fr.
Fsus
C
Cm7
3fr.
B♭
E♭2
6fr.
F2
Am
Gsus
Dm7

Emmanuel
(Hallowed Manger Ground)

340

Words and Music by
CHRIS TOMLIN and ED CASH

(to meas. 5)
2. to CHORUS
Eb/Bb Bb Eb/Bb
mf
2. What ground! Em -
CHORUS
Bb F Bb/D
man - u - el, Em - man - u -
Eb2 Bb/D Eb Bb/F
el, God in - car - nate, here to
F Bb F Bb/D
dwell. Em - man - u - el, Em - man - u -
2nd time to Coda
(to meas. 48)
Eb2 Bb/D Eb Bb/F F7
el, praise His name, Em - man - u -

B♭
E♭2/G
B♭/D
E♭2/G
mf
el.
3. The
32
VERSE 3
B♭
E♭2
F
Son of God, here, born to bleed; a crown of thorns would
36
B♭sus
B♭
B♭/D
E♭2
pierce His brow. And we be-held this Of-fer-ing, ex-
39
B♭/F
E♭2/G
Cm7
alt-ed now, the King of kings. Praise God for the hal-low-ed
42
D.S. al Coda
(to meas. 17)
Fsus
B♭
F/B♭
E♭/B♭
f
man-ger ground! Em-
45

CODA
TAG
ENDING
Gm7
Bb/D
Eb
Bb/F
F7
Bb
Eb2/G
Eb2
molto rit.
el.
Praise His
name, Em - man - u - el!
48
51
55
59

Chords Used:

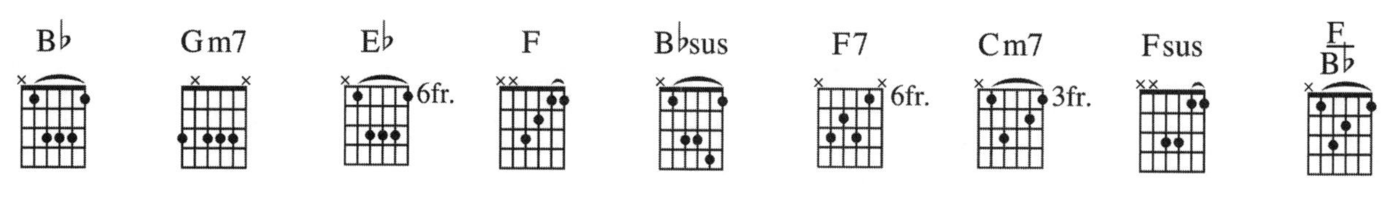
Bb
Gm7
Eb
6fr.
F
Bbsus
F7
6fr.
Cm7
3fr.
Fsus
F/Bb

Every Praise

Words and Music by
HEZEKIAH WALKER and JOHN DAVID BRATTON

1. Repeat CHORUS
E♭
F
B♭
Ev - 'ry praise, ev - 'ry praise is to our God.
13
(to meas. 9)
2. to CHORUS (Key Change)
B♭
to our God.
16
CHORUS
B
Ev - 'ry praise is to our God;
Sing Hal - le - lu - jah! to our God.
19
G♯m7
ev - 'ry word of wor - ship, with one ac - cord.
Glo - ry, Hal - le - lu - jah! is due our God.
21
E
F♯
Ev - 'ry praise, ev - 'ry praise is
23

1. Repeat CHORUS
(to meas. 19)
2. to CHORUS (Key Change)
B
to our God.
B
to our God.
25
CHORUS
C
Ev - 'ry praise is
Sing Hal - le - lu - jah!
28
to our God;
to our God.
Am7
ev - 'ry word of wor - ship, with
Glo - ry, Hal - le - lu - jah! is
30
one ac - cord.
due our God.
F
Ev - 'ry praise,
32
G
ev - 'ry praise is
1. Repeat CHORUS
(to meas. 29)
C
to our God.
34

2. to BRIDGE
BRIDGE
C
ff
to our God.
God, my
Am7
Sav - ior.
God, my
Heal - er.
Fmaj9
1., 2. Repeat BRIDGE
Dm7
God, my De - liv - er - er.
Yes, He is!
B♭
(to meas. 39)
3. to CHORUS
Dm7
B♭
Yes, He is!
Yes, He is!
Yes, He is!
Dm7
B♭
CHORUS
C
Yes, He is!
Yes, He is!
Ev - 'ry praise is

Am7
to our God;
ev - 'ry word of wor - ship, with one ac - cord.
52
VAMP
F
G
F/A
Ev - 'ry praise,
ev - 'ry praise,
ev - 'ry praise,
55
Repeat as desired (to meas. 55)
ENDING
G/B
F/A
G/B
C
G/B
F/A
G
F
ev - 'ry praise,
ev - 'ry praise,
58
G
G/B
C
ev - 'ry praise is to our God!
60

Chords Used:

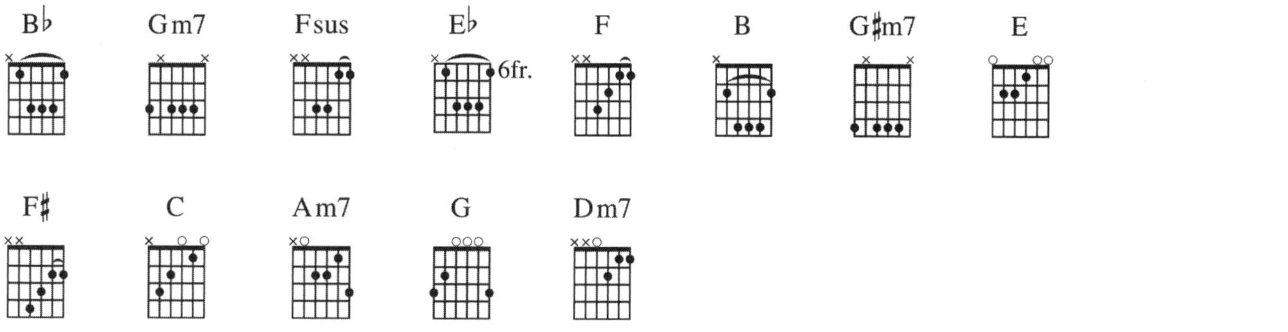
B♭
Gm7
Fsus
E♭
6fr.
F
B
G♯m7
E
F♯
C
Am7
G
Dm7

342 Forever (We Sing Hallelujah)

Words and Music by
BRIAN JOHNSON, CHRISTA BLACK GIFFORD,
GABRIEL WILSON, JENN JOHNSON,
JOEL TAYLOR, and KARI JOBE

With conviction (♩ = 72)
A♭
E♭
B♭m7
D♭2
p
VERSE 1, 2
A♭
p–mp
E♭(4)
1. The moon and stars, they wept. The morn - ing sun was
2. One fi - nal breath He gave as Heav - en looked a -
2nd time play cued notes
Fm7
D♭
dead. The Sav - ior of the world was fall - en.
- way. The Son of God was laid in dark - ness.
A♭
E♭(4)
His bod - y on the cross, His blood poured out for
A bat - tle in the grave, the war on death was

1. Repeat to VERSE 2
Fm7
Db
Ab
p
us; the weight of ev - 'ry curse up-on Him.
waged, the pow'r of hell for -
11
Eb
Bbm7
Db2
(to meas. 5)
2. to PRE-CHORUS
Db
ev - er bro - ken.
14
PRE-CHORUS
Ab
mf
Eb(4)
The ground be - gan to shake, the stone was rolled a -
18
Fm7
Db
way. His per - fect love could not be o - ver - come.
20
Ab/C
Eb(4)
Now death, where is your sting? Our res - ur-rect - ed
22

Fm7
Db
ff
King has ren - dered you de - feat - ed. For -
CHORUS
Absus
Ab
Ebsus
Eb
ev - er He is glo - ri - fied. For -
Db/F
Fm7
Ab/Db
Db
ev - er He is lift - ed high! For -
Absus
Ab
Ab/Eb
Eb
ev - er He is ris - en; He is a - live,
1. Repeat to PRE-CHORUS
(to meas. 18)
2. to INSTRUMENTAL
Fm7
Db
Fm7
He is a - live!
He is a - live!

INSTRUMENTAL
D♭
A♭sus
A♭
E♭sus
E♭
Worship Leader ad libs
35
D♭/F
Fm7
A♭/D♭
D♭
A♭sus
A♭
38
A♭/E♭
E♭
Fm7
D♭
41
INTERLUDE
A♭
E♭(4)
Fm7
D♭
(Repeat to meas. 44)
p
44
BRIDGE 1
A♭
p–mp–mf
E♭(4)
We sing Hal - le - lu - jah! We sing Hal - le - lu -
2nd time play cued notes
48

Fm7
1. Repeat BRIDGE 1 (as desired)
(to meas. 48)
D♭
- jah! We sing Hal - le-lu - jah! The Lamb has o - ver-come!
50
2. to BRIDGE 2
D♭
BRIDGE 2
A♭
mf–f
- jah! The Lamb has o - ver-come! We sing Hal - le-lu-
52
E♭(4)
Fm7
- jah! We sing Hal - le-lu - jah! We sing Hal - le-lu-
54
1. Repeat BRIDGE 2
(to meas. 53)
2. to CHORUS
D♭
D♭
- jah! The Lamb has o - ver-come! - jah! The Lamb has o - ver-come!
56
A♭/D♭
ff
CHORUS
A♭sus
A♭
For - ev - er He is
58

E♭sus E♭ D♭/F Fm7
glo - ri - fied. For - ev - er He is
60
A♭/D♭ D♭ A♭sus A♭
lift - ed high! For - ev - er He is
62
1. Repeat CHORUS
(to meas. 59)
A♭/E♭ E♭ Fm7 D♭
ris - en; He is a - live, He is a - live! For -
64
2. SONG ENDING
Fm7 D♭ A♭2
He is a - live!
67

Chords Used:

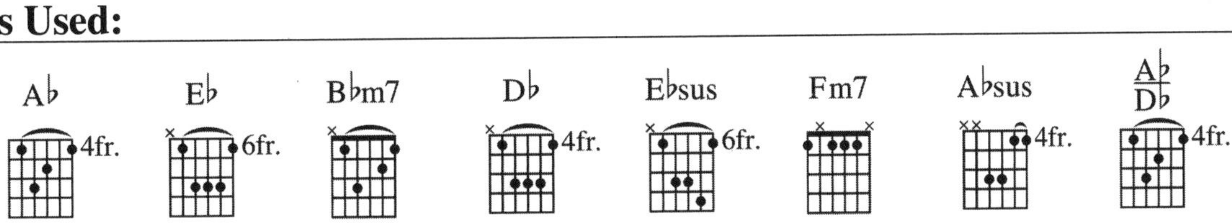
A♭
4fr.
E♭
6fr.
B♭m7
D♭
4fr.
E♭sus
6fr.
Fm7
A♭sus
4fr.
A♭/D♭
4fr.

343

God's Not Dead
(Like a Lion)

Words and Music by
DANIEL BASHTA

C
Em7
lu - tion some - how. Let love ex -
rec - tion some - how. Let hope a -
15
Dsus
G
plode and bring the dead to life,
rise and make the dark - ness hide.
18
Am7
G
C
a love so bold to bring a rev - o - lu - tion
My faith is dead; I need a res - ur - rec - tion
21
PRE-CHORUS
D(4)
some - how.
some - how.
Now I'm lost in Your free -
24
Em7
D(4)
- dom.
Oh, this
27

C
f
world I'll o - ver - come. My God's
30
CHORUS
D
not dead. He's sure-ly a-live, and He's liv - in' on the in - side,
Em7
33
D(4)
roar-ing like a li-on. My God's not dead. He's sure-ly a-live, and He's liv -
36
1. Repeat to INTRO
(to meas. 1)
2., 3. Continue CHORUS
Em7
- in' on the in - side, roar-ing like a li - on. - in' on the in - side,
39
D(4)
roar-ing like a li-on. My God's not dead. He's sure-ly a-live, and He's liv -
42

Em7
D(4)
- in' on the in - side, roar-ing like a li - on. My God's not dead. He's
2nd time to Coda
(to meas. 69)
Em7
sure-ly a-live, and He's liv - in' on the in - side, roar-ing like a li - on.
INSTRUMENTAL
G
D/F♯
Em7
C
mp
Let Heav - en
BRIDGE
G
D/F♯
mp–mf–f–ff
roar and fi - re fall;
2nd time play cued notes

Em7
come shake the ground with the sound of re -
1. Repeat BRIDGE (as desired)
(to meas. 59)
2. to CHORUS
D.S. al Coda
(to meas. 33)
Am7
Am7
viv - al. Let Heav - en viv - al. My God's
CODA
ENDING
Em7
Em7
Worship Leader ad libs (opt.)
D
roar-in' like a li - on.
1. Repeat ENDING (as desired)
(to meas. 70)
2. SONG ENDING
G
G

Chords Used:

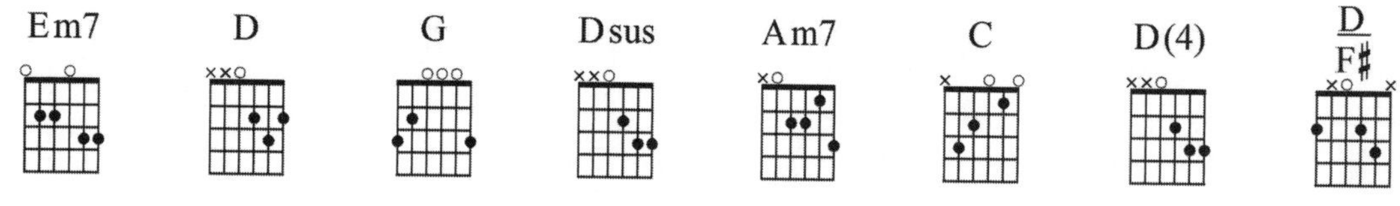
Em7
D
G
Dsus
Am7
C
D(4)
D
F♯

Hands to the Heavens

Words and Music by
BRYAN BROWN, JASON INGRAM,
KARI JOBE, and TOFER BROWN

VERSE 2, 3
Em C2 D(4) Em C2
2. We lift our eyes.
3. You are the Way,
15
G Em C2 G D
We lay our hearts be - fore You,
the Truth and Life we live for.
18
Em C2 G D/F♯ Em C2
(sing cue notes 2nd time)
ex - pect - ant here for You to move.
Oh, how we long to know You more.
21
CHORUS
D(4) C2 Em7
f
With our hands to the heav - ens, a - live in Your pres - ence, O God,
24
G Dsus C2
when You come. So, pour out Your Spir - it; we love
27

1. Repeat to VERSE 3
Em7 G Dsus
to be near You, O God, when You come.
30
(to meas. 17)
Em C2 G Em C2 G
33
2. Repeat CHORUS (to meas. 25)
3. to BRIDGE
BRIDGE
Dsus Dsus Am7
mf
With our hands Come, like a rush-
37
Em7 G2 Dsus
- ing wind. Come, light the fire a - gain.
40
1., 2. Repeat BRIDGE
Am7 Em7 Dsus
Come, like a burn - ing flame. Have Your way, have
43

(to meas. 39)
3. to CHORUS
Dsus
Your way.
Your way.
CHORUS
C2
With our hands to the heavens, a - live
Em7
G
Dsus
in Your pres-ence, O God, when You come. So, pour
C2
Em7
1. Repeat CHORUS
G
out Your Spir - it; we love to be near You, O God, when You come.
(to meas. 49)
2. to BRIDGE
Dsus
G
Dsus
With our hands when You come.

BRIDGE
Am7
ff
Em7
Come, like a rush - ing wind.
59
G2
Dsus
Am7
Come, light the fire a - gain.
Come, like a burn -
61
Em7
1. Repeat BRIDGE
(to meas. 59)
Dsus
- ing flame.
Have Your way,
have Your way.
64
2. SONG ENDING
Dsus
C2
Your way,
have Your way.
67

Chords Used:

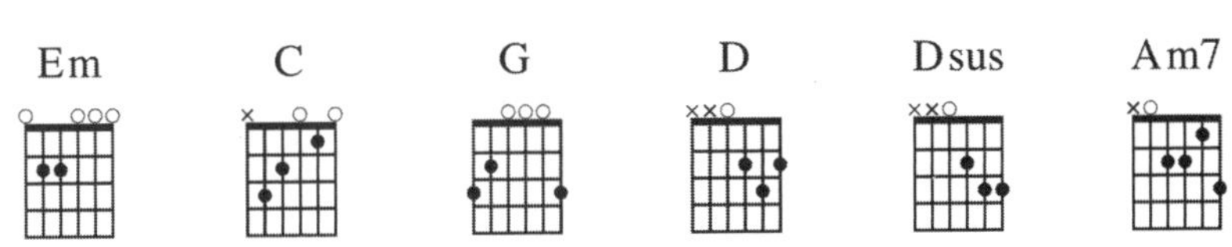
Em
C
G
D
Dsus
Am7

Healer

Words and Music by
MIKE GUGLIELMUCCI

Medium worship ballad (♩ = 78)

PRE-CHORUS
CHORUS
C
Gm7
F/A
B♭2
Gm7
B♭2
C
F
Dm7
C
B♭2
F
Dm7
C
mf–f
I trust in You; I
trust in You.
I be-lieve
You're my Heal-er; I be-lieve You are all I
need.
I be-lieve
You're my Por-tion; I be-lieve You're more than e-nough for me.
12
15
18
21
24

3rd time to Coda
(to meas. 45)
1. Repeat to VERSE
Bb2 C Bb2/D C/E Bb2 C
Je - sus, You're all I need.
27
Bb2/D C/E
(to meas. 5)
2. to BRIDGE
Bb2 C Bb2/D C/E
You
30
BRIDGE
Dm7 C/E F Dm7 C/E
mp–mf
1st x: half note accompaniment
2nd x: as written
Noth - ing is im - pos - si - ble for You; noth - ing is im - pos -
33
F Dm7 C/E
1. Repeat BRIDGE
F
- si - ble. Noth-ing is im - pos - si - ble for You.
36
Bb2 Dm7 C
(to meas. 33)
2. to CHORUS
F F/A
You hold my world in Your hands. - si - ble for You.
39

D.S. al Coda
(to meas. 17)
B♭2
Dm7
C
You hold my world in Your hands.
42
CODA
B♭2
C
B♭2/D
C/E
Gm7
F/A
more than e-nough for me.
45
ENDING
B♭2
C
F
B♭2
Je-sus, You're all I need.
48
Dm7
B♭2
F
51

Chords Used:

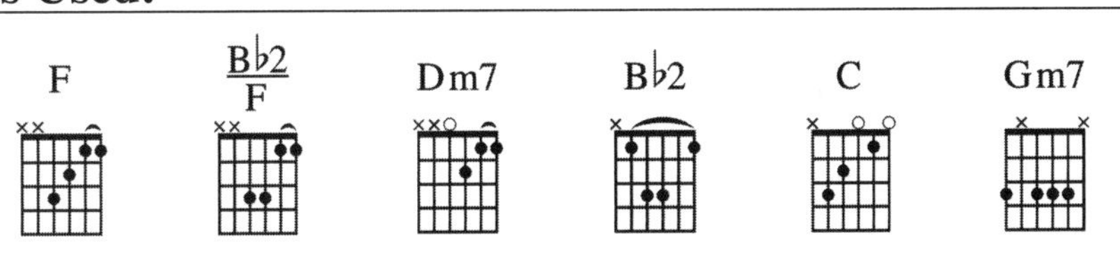
F
B♭2/F
Dm7
B♭2
C
Gm7

Holy Spirit

Words and Music by
BRYAN TORWALT and KATIE TORWALT

Worship Ballad (♩ = 72)
A(no3)
Dmaj7
p
VERSE
A(no3)
p–mf
There's noth - ing worth more
that will ev - er come close;
5
Dmaj7
no thing can com - pare.
You're our liv - ing Hope,
7
A(no3)
Dmaj7
Your pres - ence.
9

A(no3)
I've tast - ed and seen
12
Dmaj7
of the sweet - est of loves, where my heart be - comes free
14
A(no3)
and my shame is un - done
16
Dmaj7
in Your pres - ence, Lord.
18
CHORUS
A
mf–f
Ho - ly Spir - it, You are wel - come here. Come,
21

Dmaj7
Bm7
flood this place and fill the at - mos - phere. Your
23
A
Dmaj7
glo - ry, God, is what our hearts long for, to be o - ver - come by Your
25
1. Repeat to VERSE
Bm7
A
pres - ence, Lord,
Your pres - ence,
28
(to meas. 5)
2. Repeat CHORUS
(to meas. 21)
Dmaj7
Bm7
Bm7
Lord.
pres - ence, Lord.
31
3. to INTERLUDE
INTERLUDE
Bm7
A
pres - ence, Lord.
34

(opt. W.L. ad libs)
Dmaj7
Bm7
BRIDGE
A(no3)
mf
Let us be-come more a-ware of Your pres - ence.
Let us ex-per - i-ence the glo - ry of Your good - ness.
8vb
Dmaj7
A/C♯
Bm7
A/C♯
mf–f–ff
Let us be-come more a-ware of Your pres - ence.
Dmaj7
A/C♯
Bm7
A/C♯
(Repeat to m. 43 as desired)
Let us ex-per - i-ence the glo - ry of Your good - ness.

Dmaj7
A
mp
Holy Spirit, You are welcome here. Come, flood this place and fill the atmosphere. Your glory, God, is what our hearts long for, to be overcome by Your presence, Lord.
Dmaj7
Bm7
A
Dmaj7
Bm7
A(no3)
47
50
52
55

Chords Used:

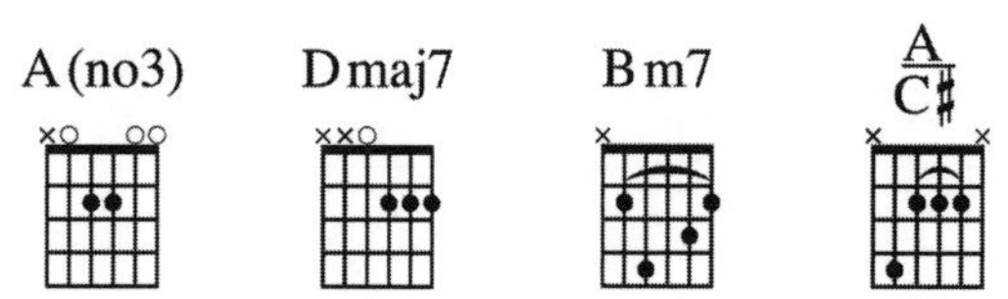
A(no3)
Dmaj7
Bm7
A/C♯

How Majestic

Words and Music by
CHRIS TOMLIN, JASON INGRAM,
KARI JOBE, and MATT REDMAN

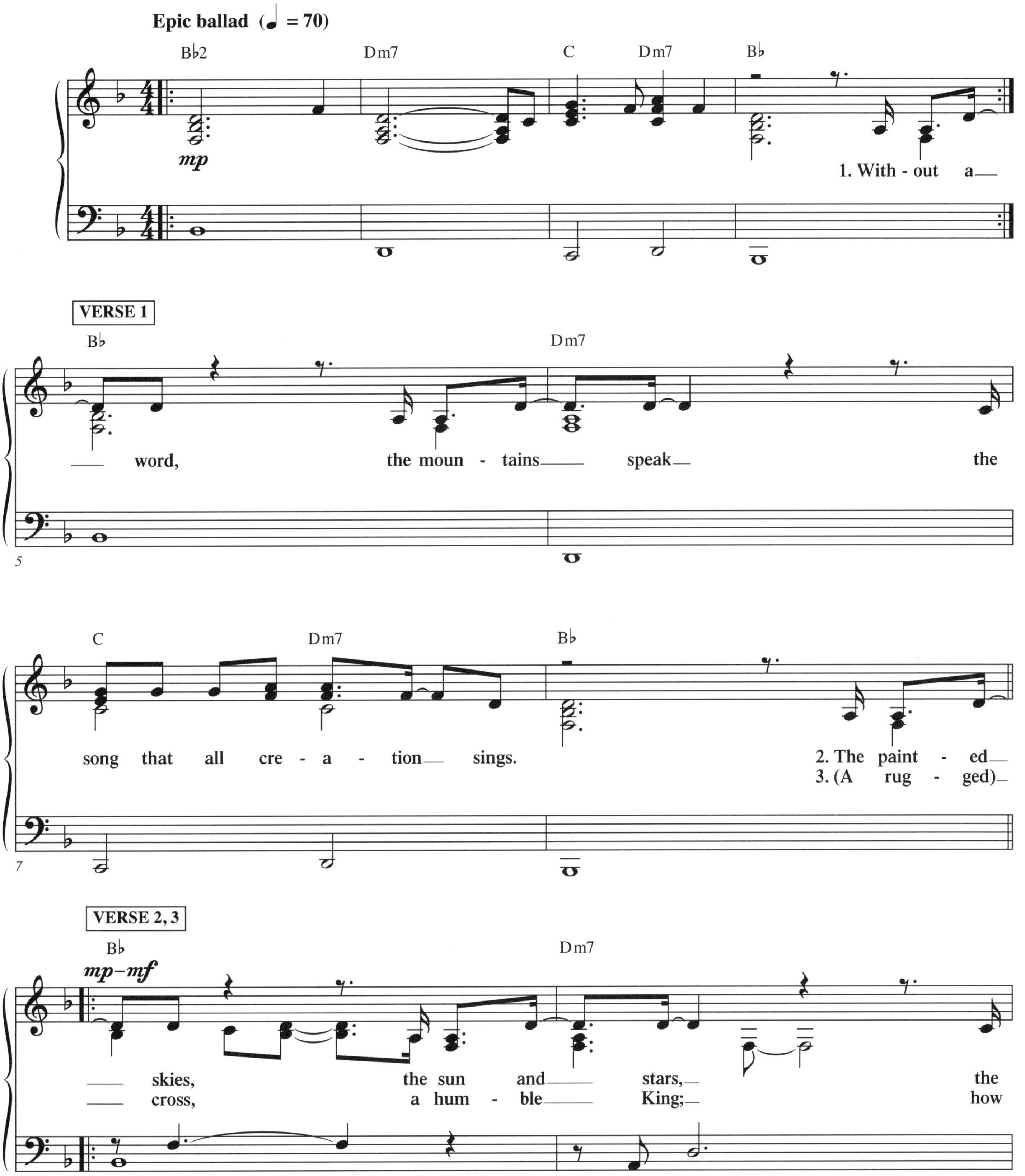

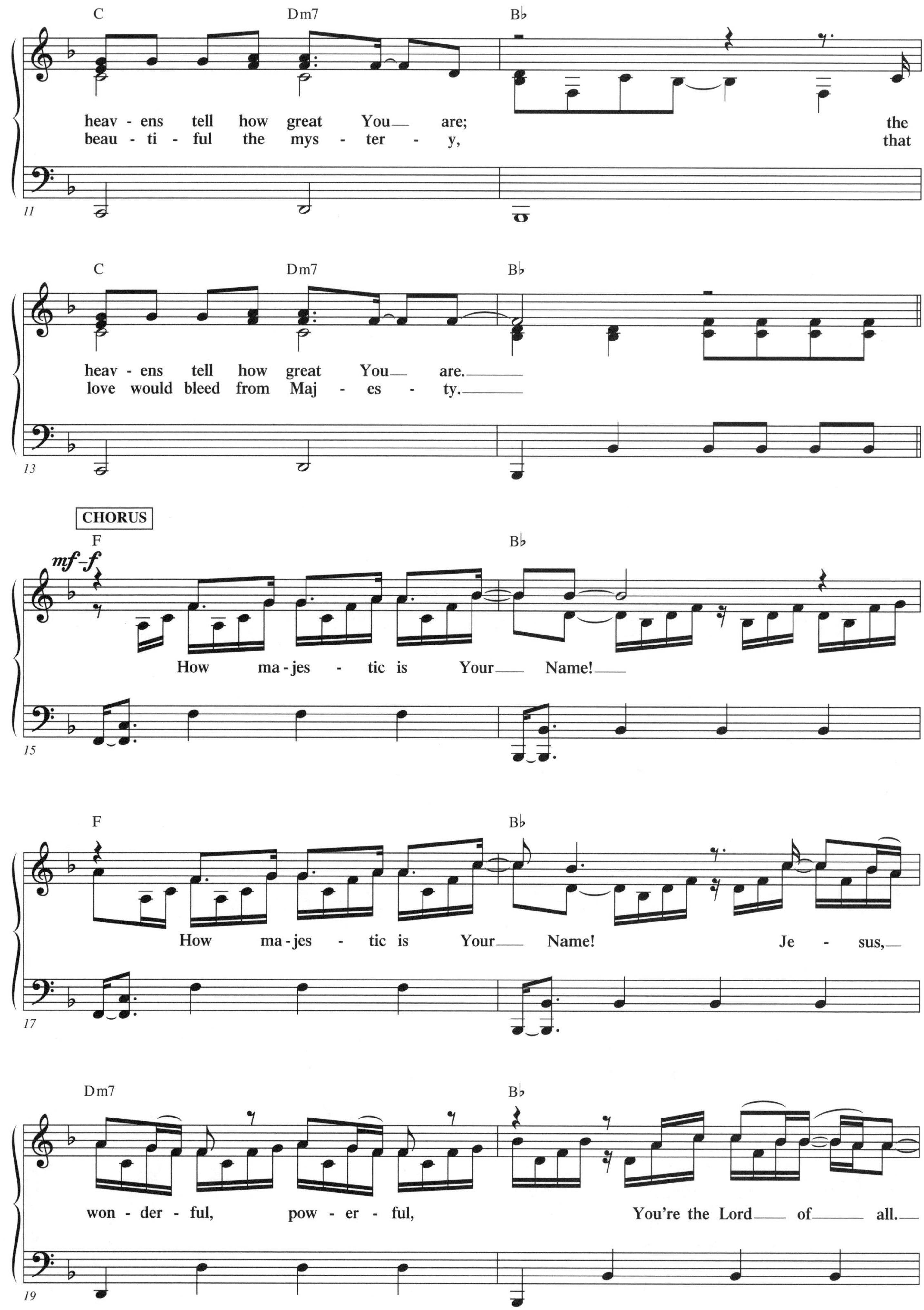
C Dm7 B♭
heav - ens tell how great You__ are; the
beau - ti - ful the mys - ter - y, that
11
C Dm7 B♭
heav - ens tell how great You__ are.__
love would bleed from Maj - es - ty.__
13
CHORUS
F B♭
mf-f
How ma - jes - tic is Your__ Name!__
15
F B♭
How ma - jes - tic is Your__ Name! Je - sus,__
17
Dm7 B♭
won - der - ful, pow - er - ful, You're the Lord__ of__ all.__
19

1. Repeat to VERSE 3
(to meas. 9)
F
B♭
How ma - jes - tic is Your Name! 3. A rug - ged
2. to BRIDGE
F
B♭
ff
How ma - jes - tic is Your Name! All
BRIDGE
C Dm7 B♭ F C Dm7
rise, all rise in high - est praise! Your Name will reign through
B♭ F C Dm7
all e - ter - ni - ty! Our Hope, our Strength, our
B♭ F C
Vic - to - ry; we bow down,

CHORUS
F
mp–ff
down at Your feet.
How ma-jes - tic is Your
32
B♭
F
Name!
How ma-jes - tic is Your
34
B♭
f
Dm7
Name!
Je - sus,
won - der - ful,
pow - er - ful,
36
B♭
F
You're the Lord of all.
How ma-jes - tic is Your
38
1. Repeat CHORUS
(to meas. 33)
2. to TAG
B♭
B♭
Name!
Name!
40

TAG
F
B♭
How ma-jes - tic is Your Name!
42
F
B♭
How ma-jes - tic is Your Name!
44
F
B♭
How ma-jes - tic is Your Name!
46
ENDING
F
B♭
F
B♭
F
Worship Leader ad lib (opt.)
(Repeat to m. 48 as desired)
mp
48

Chords Used:

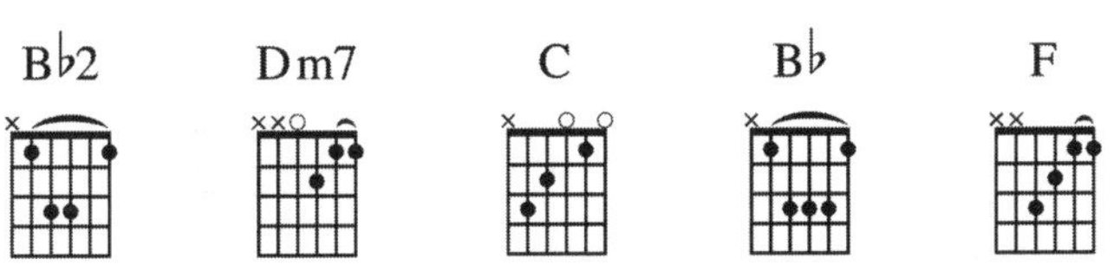
B♭2
Dm7
C
B♭
F

I Am

Words and Music by
DAVID CROWDER and ED CASH

Driving acoustic (♩ = 104)
B♭(no3)
p
VERSE 1, 2
B♭
mp
Gm7
1. There's no space that His love can't reach; there's no place where we
2. Take me in, with Your arms spread wide; take me in like an
3
Fsus
can't find peace. There's no end to a - maz - ing grace.
or - phan child. Nev - er let go, nev - er leave my side.
6
1. Repeat to VERSE 2
(to meas. 3)
2. to CHORUS
E♭2
E♭2
f
I am
9

CHORUS
B♭
Gm7
— holding on to — You. — I — am — holding
13
E♭
on to — You. — In the middle of — the storm,
16
B♭
I am hold - ing on, I am. —
18
VERSE 3
B♭
Gm7
mf
3. Love like this, — O my God, to find. — I am o - ver - whelmed; what a
21
F
f
joy di - vine! — Love like this sets our hearts — on fire. I — am —
24

CHORUS
B♭
f
Gm7
holding on to You. I am holding
28
E♭2
on to You. In the middle of the storm, I am holding on, I am.
31
1. Repeat CHORUS
(to meas. 28)
2. to BRIDGE
B♭
B♭
I am
34
B♭
B♭maj7
E♭
p
38
BRIDGE
B♭
E♭2
B♭/D
E♭2
mp–mf 1st time: Guys sing 8vb
This is my resurrection song; this is my "Hallelujah, come!"
42

1. Repeat BRIDGE
(to meas. 42)
Gm7
Fsus
E♭2
E♭(♯4)
This is why it's to You I run.
46
2. to CHORUS
Fsus
B♭
f
E♭2
You I run. There's no space that His love can't reach,
50
B♭/D
E♭2/G
Gm
there's no place where we can't find peace; there's no end to a -
53
F
mf
maz - ing grace. I am
56
CHORUS
B♭
mf–ff
Gm7
hold - ing on to You. I am hold - ing
59

1., 2. Repeat CHORUS
(to meas. 59)
E♭2
ff
on to You. In the mid-dle of the storm, I am hold - ing on, I am
62
3. to ENDING
E♭2
ENDING
B♭
mid-dle of the storm, I am hold - ing on, I am.
65
Gm7
In the
68
E♭2
B♭
mid-dle of the storm, I am hold - ing on, I am.
71

Chords Used:

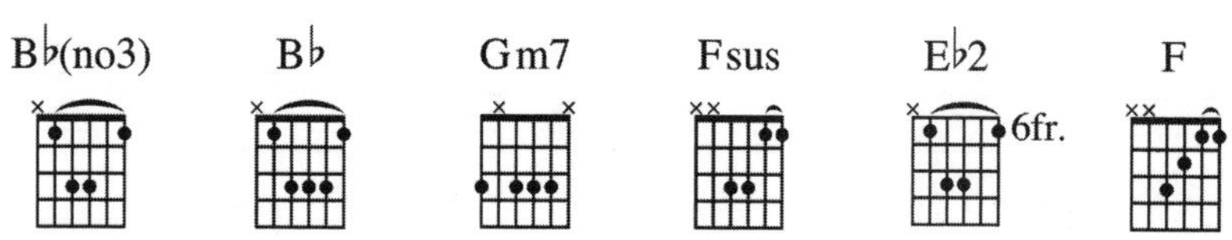
B♭(no3)
B♭
Gm7
Fsus
E♭2
6fr.
F

I Lift My Hands

Words and Music by
CHRIS TOMLIN, LOUIE GIGLIO,
and MATT MAHER

Cm7
(as written both x's)
E♭
Gm7
F
mf
let faith a-rise.
I lift my hands
CHORUS
B♭
Gm7
to be-lieve a-gain.
You are my ref - uge, You are my strength.
E♭2
B♭/D
As I pour out my heart, these things I re-mem - ber:
You are faith-
A♭
1. Repeat to VERSE 2
E♭2
mp
B♭
E♭2
- ful, God, for-ev - er.
Gm7
F(4)
(to meas. 6)
2. Repeat CHORUS
(to meas. 18)
3. to BRIDGE
E♭2
E♭2
f
2. Be still, - er.
I lift my hands - er.
Let faith a-rise,

BRIDGE
B♭
Gm7
let faith a - rise.
O - pen my eyes,
o - pen my eyes.
E♭2
B♭/D
Let faith a - rise,
let faith a - rise.
O - pen my eyes,
A♭/C
E♭2
ff
o - pen my eyes.
I lift my hands
CHORUS
B♭
Gm7
to be-lieve a - gain.
You are my ref - uge,
You are my strength.
E♭2
B♭/D
As I pour out my heart,
these things I re - mem -

1. Repeat CHORUS
(to meas. 41)
A♭/C
E♭2
- ber: You are faith - ful, God, for - ev - er. I lift my hands
46
2. to SONG ENDING
A♭
E♭2
ENDING
mp B♭ (cues = keyboard above vocal)
- ful, God; You're faith - ful, God, for - ev - er.
49
E♭2
Gm7
F(4)
B♭
Let faith a - rise,
52
E♭2
Gm7
F(4)
molto rit.
B♭
let faith a - rise.
56

Chords Used:

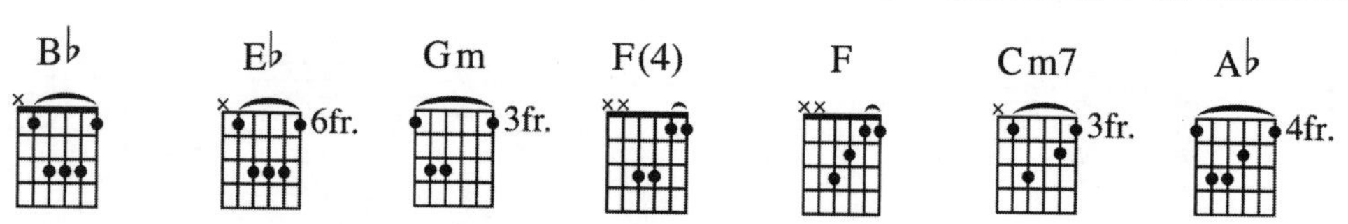
B♭
E♭
6fr.
Gm
3fr.
F(4)
F
Cm7
3fr.
A♭
4fr.

I'm Going Free
(Jailbreak)

Words and Music by
BENJI COWART, JACOB SOOTER,
and TYLER MILLER

B
E
B
D♯
free. I'm go - in' free.
free. I'm go - in' free.
13
CHORUS
C♯m7
f
A2
E
Glo - ry, glo - ry, hal - le - lu - jah! He threw my shack - les
16
B(4)
C♯m7
A2
in the sea. Glo - ry, glo - ry, hal - le - lu - jah!
19
E
1. Repeat to VERSE 2
B(4)
E (keyboard above vocal line)
Je - sus is my lib - er - ty. I'm go - in' free.
22
(to meas. 6)
2. Repeat CHORUS
(to meas. 16)
A2
E
B(4)
E
B
B(4)
mf
B(4)
2. I won't go lib - er - ty.
25

3. to BRIDGE
B(4)
E (keyboard above vocal line)
A2
E
lib - er - ty. I'm go - in' free.
29
B(4)
E/B
B(4)
mf
BRIDGE
E
A
E
I am free. I am free, in -
32
B
E/B
B
C♯m7
A2
E
deed. I am free. I am free, in -
36
B
f
E
A
E
deed. We are free, free in -
40
B
C♯m7
deed. We are free,
44

A2 E B
free in - deed.
47
CHORUS
C♯m7 A2 E
ff
Glo - ry, glo - ry, hal - le - lu - jah! He threw my shack - les
50
Last time to Coda
(to meas. 73)
B(4) C♯m7 A2
in the sea. Glo - ry, glo - ry, hal - le - lu - jah!
53
1., 3. Repeat CHORUS
(to meas. 50)
2. to VERSE 3
E B(4) E
Je - sus is my lib - er - ty. Je - sus is my
56
B(4) E (keyboard above vocal line) A2 E
lib - er - ty. I'm go - in' free.
59

B(4)
E/B
B(4)
C♯m7
A2
E
62
B(4)
E/B
B(4)
mf Slowing
VERSE 3
A
E
3. Some - day I'll fly a - way on Your a -
66
D.S. al Coda
(to meas. 50)
A
E
A
C♯m7
B(4)
fp
maz - ing grace. Your love is my jail - break. I'm go - in' free.
69
CODA
E
molto rit.
B
E
Je - sus is my lib - er - ty. I'm go - in' free!
73

Chords Used:

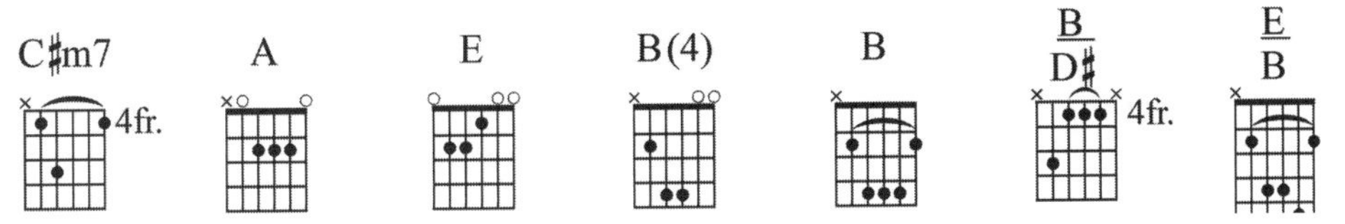
C♯m7
4fr.
A
E
B(4)
B
B/D♯
4fr.
E/B

351 Jesus, Firm Foundation

Words and Music by
BRYAN BROWN, JASON INGRAM,
and TONY WOOD

* Cue notes = keyboard part written above the vocal line.

Eb/Bb Bb Eb/Bb Gm7 F
you He has said, to you who for ref - uge to Je - sus have
cause us to stand, up - held by His mer - ci - ful, Al - might - y
10
1. Repeat to VERSE 2
(to meas. 5)
2. to CHORUS
Bb Eb/Bb Bb Eb/Bb Bb
f
fled? 2. Fear hand. How
13
CHORUS
Eb2 Bb Fsus Eb2 Bb
firm our foun - da - tion! How sure our sal -
16
Fsus Gm7 Eb2 Fsus Gm7
va - tion! And we will not be shak - en!
19
Eb2 Bb Fsus
2nd time to Coda
(to meas. 38)
Bb Eb/Bb
Je - sus, firm foun - da - tion!
22

VERSE 3
mf
3. The soul that is trust - ing in
Je - sus as Lord will press on, en - dur - ing the dark - est of storms. And
though e - ven hell should en - deav - or to shake, He'll
nev - er, no nev - er, no nev - er for - sake. He'll
nev - er, no nev - er, no nev - er for - sake. How
f
D.S. al Coda
(to meas. 16)
Bb
Eb/Bb
Eb2
Gm7
F
Fsus
25
27
30
32
35

CODA
BRIDGE
CHORUS
mf
f
Bb Eb/Bb Bb Eb/Bb Eb F
Gm7 F
Eb F Gm7 Fsus
Eb2 Bb Fsus
Eb2 Bb Fsus
tion! Age to age He stands, faithful to the end.
All may fade away, but He will remain. He will remain.
How firm our foundation! How sure our salvation! And
38
41
44
47
50

Gm7 E♭2 Fsus Gm7 E♭2 B♭
we will not be shak - en! Je - sus, firm foun -
52
Fsus Gm7 E♭2 B♭ Fsus Gm7
da - tion! Je - sus, firm foun - da - tion!
55
E♭2 B♭ Fsus B♭ E♭/B♭
Je - sus, firm foun - da - tion!
58
B♭ E♭/B♭ B♭ E♭/B♭ B♭
61

Chords Used:

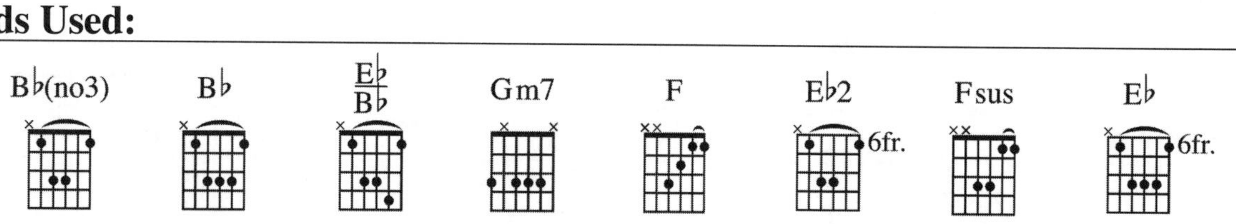
B♭(no3)
B♭
E♭/B♭
Gm7
F
E♭2
6fr.
Fsus
E♭
6fr.

Jesus, Only Jesus

352

Words and Music by
CHRIS TOMLIN, CHRISTY NOCKELS,
KRISTIAN STANFILL, MATT REDMAN,
NATHAN NOCKELS, and TONY WOOD

Gently, simply (♩ = 65)
B♭
E♭2
mp
VERSE 1, 2
B♭
1. Who has the pow'r to raise the dead? Who can
2. (Who can) make the blind to see? Who holds the
Gm7
E♭2
save us from our sin? He is our Hope, our Righ-teous -
keys that set us free? He paid it all to bring us
B♭/D
Cm7
Fsus
1. Repeat to VERSE 2
(to meas. 5)
B♭
ness; Je - sus, on-ly Je - sus.
peace; Je - sus, on-ly Je -
2. Who can
4
7
10

2. to CHORUS
CHORUS
sus. Ho - ly King, Al - might - y Lord;
saints and an - gels all a - dore. I join with them and
bow be - fore Je - sus, on - ly Je - sus.
VERSE 3
3. Who can com - mand the high - est praise? Who has the
Name a - bove all names? You stand a - lone, I stand a -

Bb/D Cm7 Fsus Bb
mazed; Je - sus, on - ly Je - sus.
30
CHORUS
Eb2 Bb/D Eb2 Bb Bb/D
Ho - ly King, Al - might - y Lord; saints and an - gels all a - dore. I
34
Eb2 Bb/D Cm7 Fsus
join with them and bow be - fore Je - sus, on - ly Je -
38
1. Opt. Repeat CHORUS (to meas. 34)
2. to BRIDGE
Bb Bb
sus. sus.
41
BRIDGE
Eb2 Bb/D Eb2
You will com - mand the high - est praise. Yours is the Name
44

B♭/D
Cm7
B♭/D
a - bove all names.
You stand a - lone,
I stand a - mazed;
47
1. Repeat BRIDGE
(to meas. 44)
2. TAG ENDING
E♭2
Fsus
B♭
Je - sus, on - ly Je - sus.
Je - sus, on - ly Je -
50
Gm7
E♭2
Fsus
Gm7
sus.
Je - sus, on - ly Je - sus.
53
SONG ENDING
Opt. Repeat to CHORUS (Extended Version)
(to meas. 34)
E♭2
Fsus
B♭
B♭
Je - sus, on - ly Je - sus.
sus.
56

Chords Used:

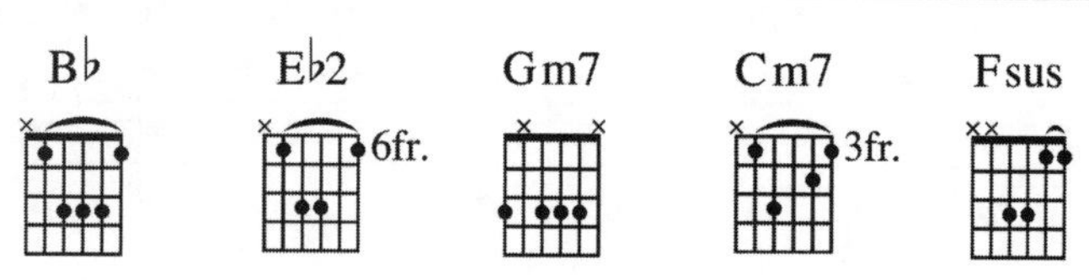
B♭
E♭2
6fr.
Gm7
Cm7
3fr.
Fsus

Joy to the World
(Unspeakable Joy)

353

Words and Music by
CHRIS TOMLIN, ED CASH,
GEORGE FRIDERIC HANDEL,
ISAAC WATTS, and MATT GILDER

B♭
Gm7
F
room, and heav'n and na - ture sing, and heav'n and na - ture sing,
plains re - peat the sound - ing joy, re - peat the sound - ing joy,
16
E♭
Cm7
Fsus
and heav'n, and heav'n and na - ture
re - peat, re - peat the sound - ing
20
1. Repeat to VERSE 2
(to meas. 5)
B♭
E♭
B♭
E♭
f
sing.
24
2. to CHORUS
B♭
joy.
28
CHORUS
E♭
B♭
f
Joy, un-speak - a - ble joy! An o - ver-flow-
32

F
E♭
- ing well,
no tongue can tell!
36
E♭
B♭
Joy,
un - speak - a - ble joy!
It ris - es in
40
F
Cm
E♭
my soul,
nev - er lets me go!
44
VERSE 3
C
F
G
Am7
mf
3. He rules the world with truth and grace, and
48
F
G
Am7
makes the na - tions prove the
52

F C/E F
glo - ries of His righ - teous -
C/E Am7
ness and won - ders of His love, and
G F
won - ders of His love, and won - ders,
Dm Gsus C
won - ders of His love.
CHORUS
F C
Joy, un - speak - a - ble joy! An o - ver - flow -

G F
- ing well, no tongue can tell!
73
F C
Joy, un-speak-a - ble joy! It ris-es in
77
G Dm
my soul, nev - er lets me go!
81
F C F C F
84
C F C
88

Chords Used:

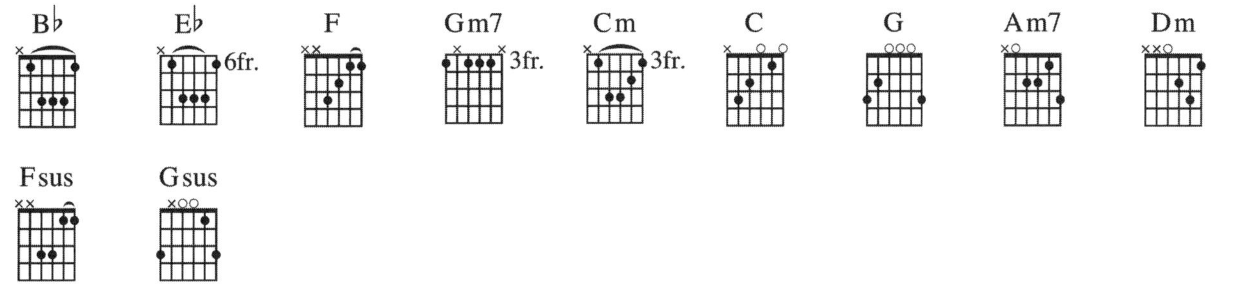
B♭
E♭
6fr.
F
Gm7
3fr.
Cm
3fr.
C
G
Am7
Dm
Fsus
Gsus

Keeper of My Heart

Words and Music by
CHRIS TOMLIN, JASON INGRAM,
and KARI JOBE

A(4) Bm7 G D A(4)
o - ver me. You nev - er fail me, God.
o - ver me. You've nev - er failed me, God.
12
CHORUS
Bm7 G2
f
I lift my eyes, I lift up eyes up, Mak-er of the heav-
15
D A(4)
- ens, Keep-er of my heart.
17
Bm7 G2
I lift my hands, I lift my hands up; stand-ing in Your pres-
19
1. Repeat to VERSE 2
(to meas. 5)
2. Repeat CHORUS
D A(4) D
- ence, You are nev - er far.
- ence, You are nev - er far.
21

(to meas. 15)
3. to BRIDGE
A(4)
D
A(4)
- ence, You are nev - er far.
Keep-er of my heart.
Bm7
G2
D
Keep-er of my heart,
Je - sus, You are.
BRIDGE
A(4)
mf
G2 1st x: more simply
2nd x: as written
My strength, Your nev-er - end - ing love.
A
G2
I know You have o - ver - come.
A
G/B
A
I'll sing when all is said and done, my
24
27
30
32
34

1. Repeat BRIDGE
(to meas. 31)
2. to CHORUS
G Bm7 A(4) D
G Bm7 A(4)
Hope, my on - ly Hope. My Hope, my on - ly Hope.
37
CHORUS
Bm7 G2
f
I lift my eyes, I lift up eyes up, Mak - er of the heav -
41
D A(4)
- ens, Keep - er of my heart.
43
Bm7 G2
I lift my hands, I lift my hands up; stand - ing in Your pres -
45
1. Repeat CHORUS
(to meas. 41)
D A(4)
- ence, You are nev - er far.
47

2. to TAG
D
A(4)
- ence, You are nev - er far. Keep - er of my heart.
49
TAG
Bm7
G2
D
Keep-er of my heart, Je - sus, You are.
51
1. Repeat TAG
(to meas. 51)
2. SONG ENDING
A(4)
A(4)
Keep-er of my heart. Keep-er of my heart.
54
Bm7
Keep-er of my heart.
56

Chords Used:

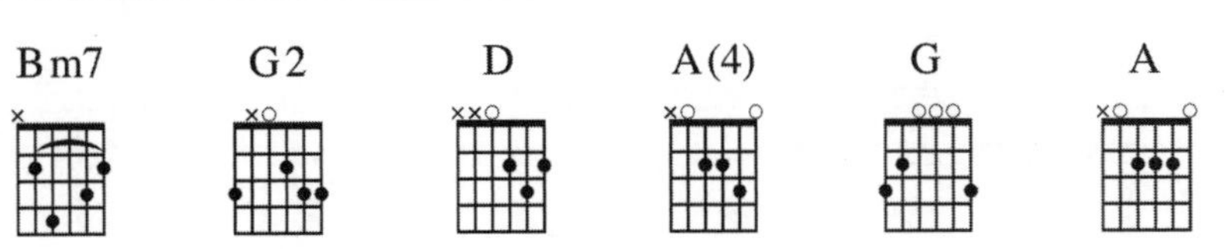
Bm7
G2
D
A(4)
G
A

Lay Me Down

Words and Music by
CHRIS TOMLIN, JASON INGRAM,
JONAS MYRIN, and MATT REDMAN

2. to CHORUS
A
(opt. 8va 2nd time)
F♯m7
I will bring a sac - rifice.
Take this life and let it shine.
E
D2
A
CHORUS
D2
f
I lay me down; I'm not my own, I be - long to You a - lone.
A
E
F♯m7
E
D2
A
Lay me down, lay me down.
E
Oh!
D2
Hand on my

A
E
F♯m7
E
heart, this much is true: there's no life a - part from
28
D2
A
E
3rd time to Coda
(to meas. 66)
You. Lay me down, lay me down.
31
1. Repeat to VERSE 3
F♯m7
E
G♯
A
34
(to meas. 5)
2. to BRIDGE
D2
3. Let - ting go Oh! Lay me
38
A
E
down, lay me down.
41

A(no3)
It will be my
BRIDGE
A2
mf–f
joy to say, "Your will, Your way." It will be my
F♯m7
joy to say, "Your will, Your way." It will be my
Esus
joy to say, "Your
D2
will, Your way,
A2
al - ways."
44
48
51
54
58

1. Repeat BRIDGE
(to meas. 48)
2. to CHORUS
Esus
D.S. al Coda
(to meas. 19)
It will be my
62
CODA
TAG
E
D2
A
Oh!
Lay me down, lay me
66
E
1. Repeat TAG
(to meas. 67)
2. to ENDING
ENDING
F♯m7
down.
Oh!
69
E
G♯
1. Repeat ENDING
(to meas. 72)
2. SONG ENDING
A
A
73

Chords Used:

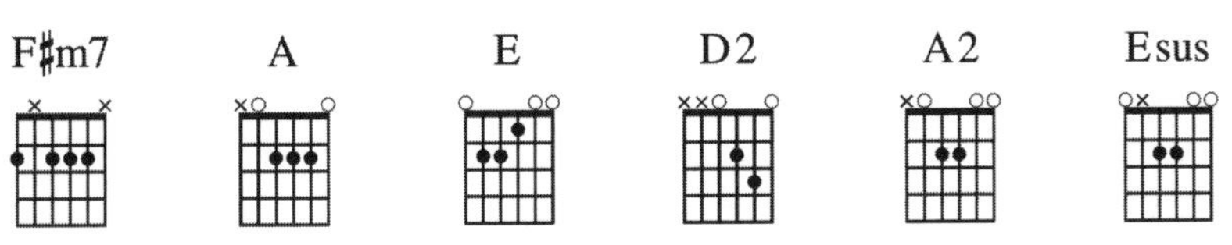
F♯m7
A
E
D2
A2
Esus

356 Lord, I Need You

Words and Music by
CHRISTY NOCKELS, DANIEL CARSON,
JESSE REEVES, KRISTIAN STANFILL,
and MATT MAHER

With resolve (♩ = 74)

B♭
E♭2
B♭
E♭2
mp
VERSE 1
B♭
mp
B♭
E♭2
B♭
Fsus
A
1. Lord, I come, I con - fess. Bow - ing
4
Gm7
Fsus
E♭2
here, I find my rest. And with - out
7
B♭
E♭2
B♭
You, I fall a - part. You're the
9

B♭/F F E♭2
One that guides my heart.
11
CHORUS
B♭ E♭2
Lord, I need You, oh, I
13
B♭ Fsus/A Gm7 E♭2
need You. Ev - 'ry hour I
15
B♭ F(4) F(4)/E♭ B♭/D E♭2
need You. My one De - fense, my
17
B♭/F E♭/G B♭/F F
Righ - teous - ness, O God, how I need
19

Bb Eb2 Bb
mf
You. 2. Where sin runs
VERSE 2
Bb Eb2 Bb Fsus/A
deep, Your grace is more. Where grace is
Gm7 Fsus Eb2
found is where You are. And where You
Bb Eb2 Bb
are, Lord, I am free. Ho - li -
Bb/F F Eb2
- ness is Christ in me. Where You

Bb Eb2 Bb
are, Lord, I am free. Ho - li -
31
Bb/F F Bb
- ness is Christ in me.
33
CHORUS
Bbsus Bb Eb2
f
Lord, I need You, oh, I
35
Bb Fsus/A Gm7 Eb2 Bb F Eb2
need You. Ev - 'ry hour I need You. My
37
2nd time to Coda (to meas. 58)
Bb/D Eb2 Bb/F Eb2/G Bb/F F
one De-fense, my Righ - teous-ness, O God, how I need
40

BRIDGE
B♭ B♭sus sub. mp E♭ B♭/D Fsus
You. So teach my song to rise to
Gm7 B♭/D E♭2
You when temp - ta - tion comes my way. And when I
B♭/D Fsus Gm7 E♭2 Fsus
can - not stand, I'll fall on You. Je - sus, You're my Hope and
B♭ E♭2 B♭/D Fsus Gm7
Stay. And when I can - not stand I'll fall on You.
E♭2 Fsus B♭ B♭sus
mf f
D.S. al Coda
(to meas. 36)
Je - sus, You're my Hope and Stay. Lord, I
43
46
49
52
55

CODA
CHORUS
B♭ B♭sus sub. mp B♭
You. Lord, I need You, oh, I
F/A Gm7 E♭2 B♭ F
need You. Ev - 'ry hour I need You. My
B♭/D E♭2 B♭/F E♭/G B♭/F F B♭
one De-fense, my Righ - teous-ness, O God, how I need You. My
B♭/D E♭2 B♭/F E♭/G B♭/F molto rit. F B♭
one De-fense, my Righ - teous-ness, O God, how I need You.

Chords Used:

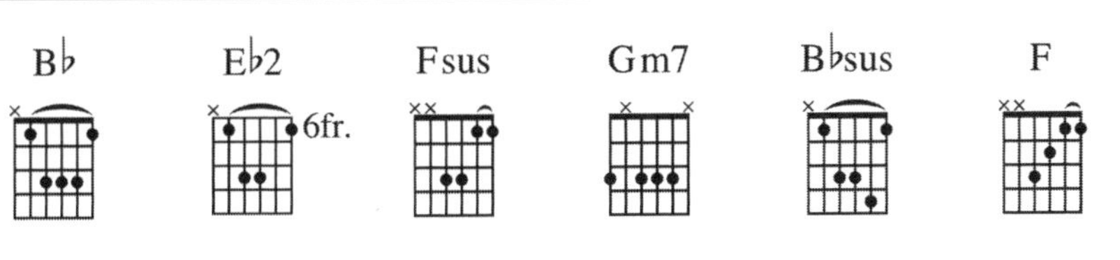
B♭
E♭2
6fr.
Fsus
Gm7
B♭sus
F

Love Came Down

Words and Music by
BRIAN JOHNSON, IAN McINTOSH,
JENN JOHNSON, JEREMY RIDDLE,
and JEREMY EDWARDSON

D♭maj9
A♭
A♭sus
A♭
lift these hands in faith; I will be-lieve. I re-
11
CHANNEL
B♭m7
A♭/C
E♭(4)
B♭m7
A♭/C
mind my-self of all that You've done and the life I have be-cause of Your Son.
13
CHORUS
D♭2
E♭(4)
A♭
mf
A♭/D♭
Love came down and res-cued me. Love came down and set me free.
16
Fm7
E♭(4)
D♭2
I am Yours, I am for-ev-er Yours.
19
A♭
A♭/D♭
Moun-tain high or val-ley low, I sing out and re-mind my soul
21

Fm7
Eb(4)
Db2
mp
I am Yours, I am for-ev-er Yours.
2. When my
VERSE 2
Dbmaj9
Fm7
Eb(4)
heart is filled with hope, ev-'ry prom-ise comes my way, when I
Dbmaj9
Ab
Ebsus/G
feel Your hands of grace rest up-on me, stay-ing
Dbmaj9
Fm7
Eb(4)
des-p'rate for You, God, stay-ing hum-bled at Your feet, I will
Dbmaj9
Ab
lift these hands and praise. I will be-lieve. I re-

CHANNEL
B♭m7
A♭/C
E♭sus
E♭
mind my-self of all that You've done
and the life I have be-cause of Your Son.
34
CHORUS
D♭2
E♭(4)
A♭
A♭/D♭
Love came down and res-cued me. Love came down and set me free.
37
Fm7
I am Yours, I am for-ev-er Yours.
40
Moun-tain high or val-ley low, I sing out and re-mind my soul
42
I am Yours, I am for-ev-er Yours. I am Yours,
44

BRIDGE
A♭
ff
A♭/D♭
I am Yours. All my days,
Fm7
E♭(4)
D♭2
Jesus, I am Yours. I am Yours,
A♭
A♭/D♭
I am Yours. All my days,
Fm7
E♭(4)
D♭2
I am Yours.
A♭
mp
A♭/D♭
Love came down and rescued me. Love came down and set me free.

Fm7 E♭(4) D♭2
I am Yours, I am for - ev - er Yours.
56
A♭ A♭/D♭
mf
Moun - tain high or val - ley low, I sing out and re - mind my soul.
58
Fm7 E♭(4) D♭2
I am Yours, I am for - ev - er Yours.
60
CHORUS
A♭ A♭/D♭
ff
Love came down and res - cued me. Love came down and set me free.
62
Fm7 E♭(4) D♭2
I am Yours, I am for - ev - er Yours.
64

A♭
A♭/C
A♭/D♭
Mountain high or valley low, I sing out and remind my soul
Fm7
E♭(4)
D♭2
I am Yours, I am forever Yours.
ENDING
Fm7
mf
E♭(4)
D♭2
(opt. Worship Leader ad libs)
Fm7
E♭(4)
D♭2
D♭maj9
mp

Chords Used:

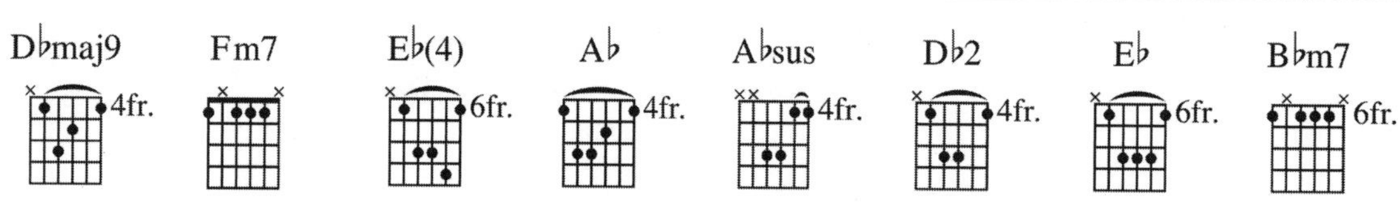

D♭maj9
4fr.
Fm7
E♭(4)
6fr.
A♭
4fr.
A♭sus
4fr.
D♭2
4fr.
E♭
6fr.
B♭m7
6fr.

Man of Sorrows 358

Words and Music by
BROOKE LIGERTWOOD and MATT CROCKER

With emotion (♩ = 72)
mp
VERSE 1, 2, 3
mp–mf
1. Man of Sor - rows, Lamb of God, by His own be - trayed. The sin of man and wrath of God has been on Je - sus laid.
2. Si - lent as He stood ac - cused, beat - en, mocked, and scorned, bow - ing to the Fa - ther's will, He
3. Sent of Heav - en, God's own Son, to pur - chase and re - deem and re - con-cile the ver - y ones who
1. Repeat to VERSE 2
(to meas. 5)
D G A Bm
5
8
11

2. 3. to CHORUS
G A D
mf–f
took a crown of thorns.
nailed Him to that tree.
Oh, that
14
CHORUS
Bm G D A Bm G
rug - ged cross, my sal - va - tion, where Your love poured out o - ver
17
A G D A/C♯ Bm
me; now my soul cries out, "Hal - le - lu - jah! Praise and
20
3rd time to Coda (to meas. 38)
1. Repeat to VERSE 3
(to meas. 5)
G A D
hon - or un - to Thee."
23
2. to BRIDGE
D
BRIDGE
Bm G D A
mp–mf
Thee." Now my debt is paid; it is paid in full by the
(2nd time play cued notes)
26

Bm G D A Bm G
pre - cious blood that my Je - sus spilled. Now the curse of sin has no
30
D A
1. Repeat BRIDGE
(to meas. 28)
Bm G D A
mf
hold on me. Whom the Son sets free, oh, is free in - deed! Now my
33
2. to CHORUS
Bm G D A
f
D.S. al Coda
(to meas. 17)
Son sets free, oh, is free in - deed! Oh, that
36
CODA
D
VERSE 4
D
mp
Thee."
4. See, the stone is
38
G D G D A
rolled a - way; be - hold the emp - ty tomb.
41

Hal - le - lu - jah, God be praised! He's ris - en from the grave!
CHORUS
Oh, that rug - ged cross, my sal - va - tion, where Your love poured out o - ver me;
now my soul cries out, "Hal - le - lu - jah! Praise and hon - or un - to Thee.
Praise and hon - or un - to Thee."
Bm G Bm G A D Bm G D A Bm G A G D A/C♯ Bm G A D G A D
f
ff
44
47
49
52
55

Chords Used:

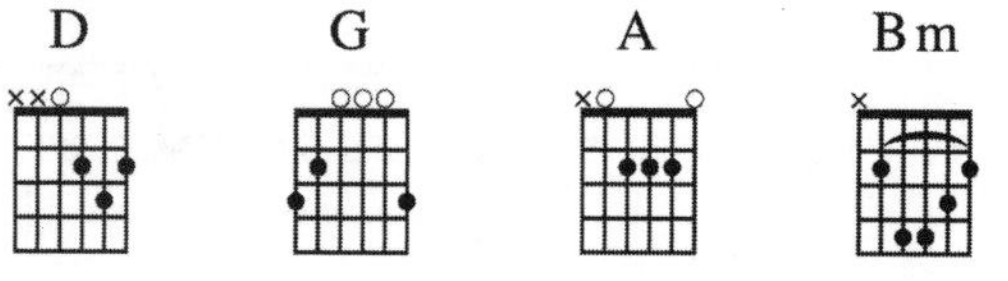
D
G
A
Bm

My Heart Is Yours

Words and Music by
BRETT YOUNKER, DANIEL CARSON,
JASON INGRAM, KRISTIAN STANFILL,
JUDSON W. VAN DeVENTER,
and WINFIELD S. WEEDEN

(to meas. 6)
2. to CHORUS
E D2 F♯m7 E
I Je - sus,
D2 F♯m7 E
Je - sus.
CHORUS
mf
D2
My heart is Yours, my
Esus D2 F♯m7 Esus
heart is Yours. Take it all, take it all, my life in Your hands. My
D2 Esus D2
heart is Yours, my heart is Yours. Take it all, take it all, my
F♯m7 E
life in Your hands.
sub. f
2. I

VERSE 2
D2 A/C♯ E F♯m7 D2 F♯m7
lay down my life; I take up my cross, Je - sus.
28
E D2 A/C♯ E F♯m7
For You are my God whatever the cost,
31
D2 F♯m7 E D2 F♯m7
Je - sus, Oh, Je - sus.
34
CHORUS
E D2 Esus
My heart is Yours, my heart is Yours. Take it
37
D2 F♯m7 Esus
all, take it all, my life in Your hands. My
40

D2
Esus
heart is Yours; Lord, my heart is Yours. Take it
42
D2
F♯m7
E
all, take it all, my life in Your hands. Take it
44
D2
F♯m
E
ff
all, take it all, my life in Your hands. And
46
BRIDGE
A
E
F♯m7
all to Je - sus I sur-ren - der. All to You I
49
E
A
A
E
free - ly give. Oh, I will ev - er love and trust You;
52

1. Repeat BRIDGE
(to meas. 49)
2. to CHORUS
F♯m7 D2 E A F♯m7 D2
in Your pres - ence I will live. And in Your pres - ence
E D2
CHORUS
mp
D2
I will live. My heart is Yours, my
E(4) D2 F♯m7 E(4)
mf
heart is Yours. Take it all, take it all, my life in Your hands. My
D2 E(4) D2
heart is Yours, my heart is Yours. Take it all, take it all, my
F♯m7 E(4) D2
life in Your hands. Take it all, take it all, my

TAG
F♯m7
E(4)
ff
D2
life in Your hands. My heart is Yours, my
70
E(4)
D2
heart is Yours. Take it all, take it all, my
72
1. Repeat TAG (as desired)
(to meas. 71)
2. SONG ENDING
F♯m7
E(4)
F♯m7
E(4)
life in Your hands. My life in Your hands. Take it
74
D2
F♯m7
molto rit.
E
all, take it all, my life in Your hands.
76

Chords Used:

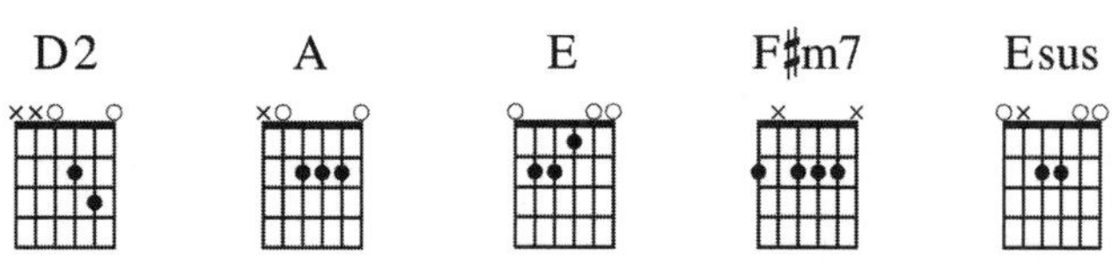
D2
A
E
F♯m7
Esus

Not for a Moment (After All)

Words and Music by
MEREDITH ANDREWS, JACOB SOOTER,
and MIA FIELDES

Medium rock (♩ = 71)
A♭maj7
E♭
B♭(4)
mp
VERSE 1
1. You were reach - ing through the storm,
Cm7
walk - ing on the wa - ter,
e - ven when I could not see.
In the mid - dle of it all,
when I

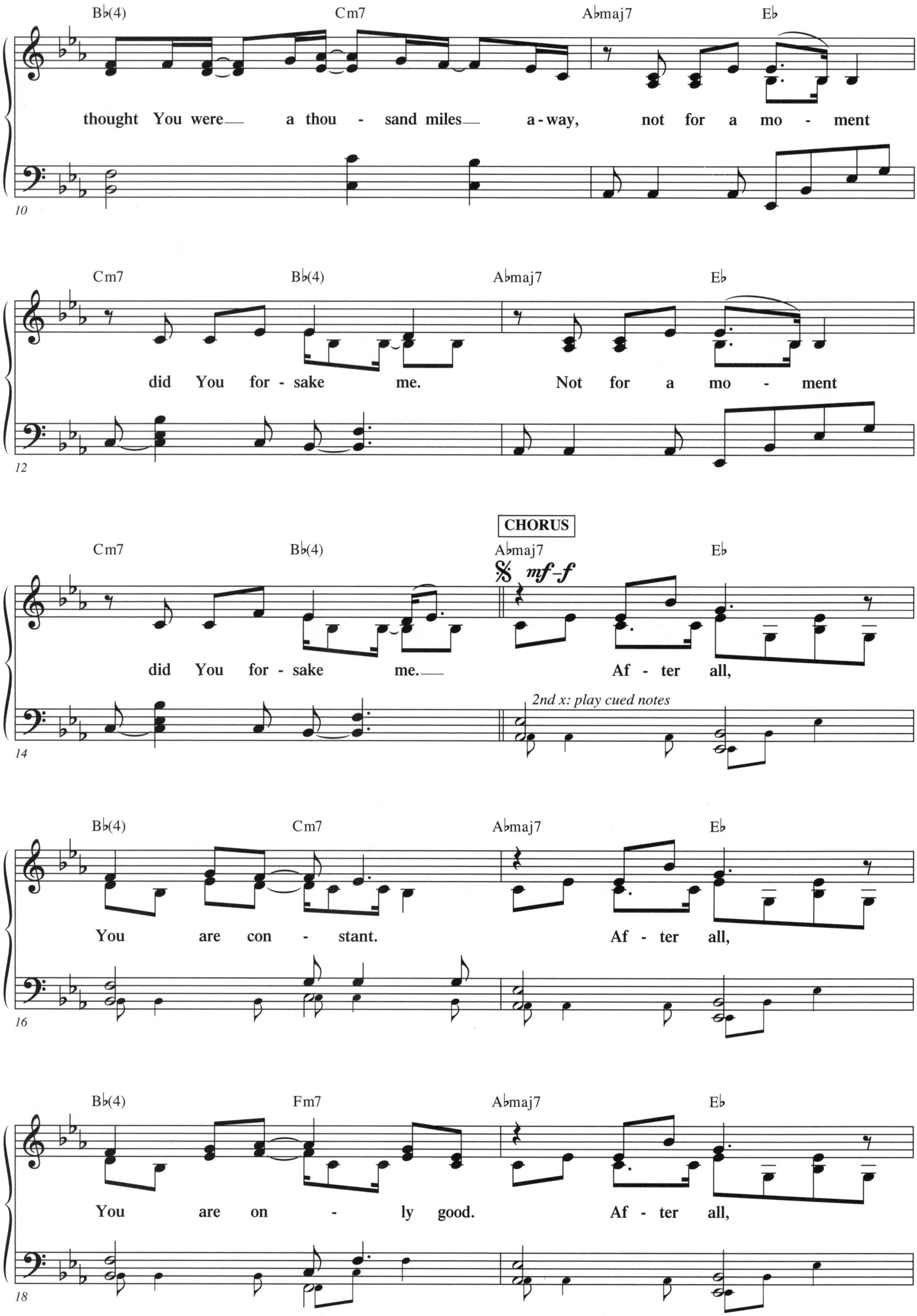
B♭(4) Cm7 A♭maj7 E♭
thought You were a thou - sand miles a-way, not for a mo - ment
10
Cm7 B♭(4) A♭maj7 E♭
did You for - sake me. Not for a mo - ment
12
CHORUS
Cm7 B♭(4) A♭maj7 E♭
mf–f
did You for - sake me. Af - ter all,
2nd x: play cued notes
14
B♭(4) Cm7 A♭maj7 E♭
You are con - stant. Af - ter all,
16
B♭(4) Fm7 A♭maj7 E♭
You are on - ly good. Af - ter all,
18

2nd time to Coda
(to meas. 33)
Cm7 B♭(4) A♭maj7 E♭ Cm7 B♭(4)
You are sov - 'reign. Not for a mo - ment will You for-sake me.
20
A♭maj7 E♭ B♭
mf
2. You were sing -
23
VERSE 2
A♭maj7 E♭ B♭ Cm7
- ing in the dark, whis - per - ing Your prom - ise,
25
A♭maj7 E♭ B♭
e - ven when I could not hear. I was
27
A♭maj7 E♭ B♭ Cm7
held in Your arms, car - ried for a thou - sand miles to show
29

D.S. al Coda
(to meas. 15)
A♭maj7 E♭ Cm7 B♭sus B♭
not for a mo - ment did You for - sake me.
31
CODA
Cm7 B♭(4) A♭maj7 E♭
will You for - sake me. Not for a mo - ment
33
BRIDGE
Cm7 B♭(4) A♭maj7 E♭
will You for - sake me. And ev - 'ry step, ev - 'ry
35
Cm7 B♭(4) A♭maj7 E♭
breath, You are there; ev - 'ry tear, ev - 'ry
37
Cm7 B♭(4) A♭maj7 E♭
cry, ev - 'ry pray'r. In my hurt, at my worst,
39

Cm7 Bb(4) Abmaj7 Eb Cm7 Bb(4)
when my world falls down, not for a mo - ment will You for - sake me.
41
Abmaj7 Eb Bb(4)
mp
f
E - ven in the dark, e - ven when it's hard, You will nev - er
44
Abmaj7 Eb Bb(4)
CHORUS
Abmaj7 Eb
ff
leave me. Af - ter all,
46
Bb(4) Cm7 Abmaj7 Eb Bb(4) Fm7
You are con - stant. Af - ter all, You are on - ly good.
49
Abmaj7 Eb Cm7 Bb(4)
Af - ter all, You are sov - 'reign.
52

TAG
A♭maj7
E♭
Cm7
B♭(4)
Not for a mo - ment will You for - sake me.
54
A♭maj7
E♭
Cm7
B♭(4)
Not for a mo - ment will You for - sake me.
56
A♭maj7
E♭
Cm7
B♭(4)
ENDING
A♭maj7
E♭
mp
(Keyboard above vocal)
Not for a mo - ment will You for-sake me.
58
B♭(4)
B♭
A♭maj7
E♭
B♭
61

Chords Used:

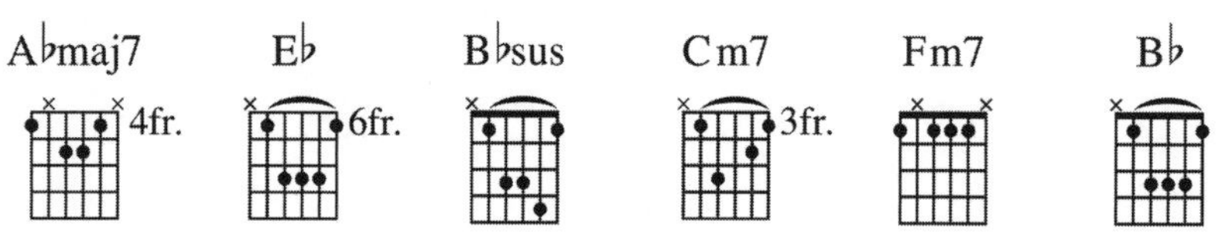
A♭maj7
4fr.
E♭
6fr.
B♭sus
Cm7
3fr.
Fm7
B♭

Oceans
(Where Feet May Fail)

361

Words and Music by
JOEL HOUSTON, MATT CROCKER,
and SALOMON LIGTHELM

B♭
A♭2
deep, ♬ my faith will stand.
failed and You won't start now.
11
CHORUS
A♭2 E♭ B♭(4) A♭2 E♭
mf
And I will call up-on Your Name and keep my eyes a-bove the
13
B♭(4) A♭2 E♭
waves. When o - ceans rise my soul will rest in Your em -
16
1. Repeat to VERSE 2
(to meas. 5)
B♭(4) A♭2 B♭ Cm
brace, for I am Yours, and You are mine.
18
2. to BRIDGE 1
BRIDGE 1
A♭2 B♭ Cm
mp
Yours, and You are mine. Spir-it, lead me where my trust
21

A♭2
E♭
is with - out bor - ders. Let me walk up - on the wa - ters wher -
24
B♭(4)
Cm
ev - er You would call me. Take me deep - er than my feet
26
A♭2
E♭
could ev - er wan - der, and my faith will be made strong - er in the pres -
28
BRIDGE 2
B♭(4)
A♭2
mf
- ence of my Sav - ior. Spir - it, lead me where my trust
30
E♭
B♭(4)
is with - out bor - ders. Let me walk up - on the wa - ters, wher -
32

Fm7
A♭2
ev - er You would call me. Take me deep - er than my feet
34
E♭
B♭(4)
could ev - er wan - der, and my faith will be made strong - er in the pres-
36
BRIDGE 3
Fm7
Cm
B♭
f
- ence of my Sav - ior. Spir - it, lead me where my trust
38
E♭
B♭(4)
is with - out bor - ders. Let me walk up - on the wa - ters, wher -
40
Fm7
Cm
B♭
ev - er You would call me. Take me deep - er than my feet
42

E♭
B♭(4)
could ev - er wan - der, and my faith will be made strong - er in the pres-
44
CHORUS
Fm7
A♭2
mp
E♭
B♭(4)
- ence of my Sav - ior. And I will call up-on Your Name,
46
A♭2
E♭
B♭(4)
A♭2
E♭
and keep my eyes a-bove the waves. My soul will rest in Your em-
49
B♭(4)
A♭2
B♭(4)
Cm
brace. I am Yours, and You are mine.
52

Chords Used:

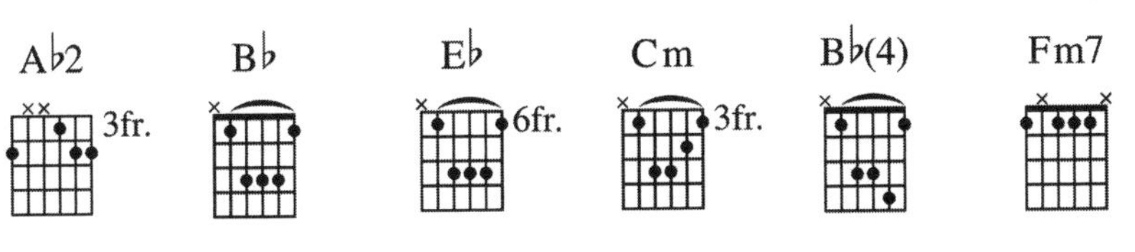
A♭2
3fr.
B♭
E♭
6fr.
Cm
3fr.
B♭(4)
Fm7

Only King Forever

Words and Music by
CHRIS BROWN, MACK BROCK,
STEVEN FURTICK, and WADE JOYE

Gm
our rock, the on - ly sol - id ground, as na -
in love and jus - tice You will reign, and ev -
Eb
Bb
- tions rise and fall.
- 'ry knee will bow.
Bb
Bbsus
Bb
King - doms once strong, now shak - en; but we trust for -
We bring our ex - pec - ta - tions; our hope is
Gm
Eb
ev - er in Your Name, the Name of Je - sus.
an - chored in Your Name, the Name of Je - sus.
Bb
Gm
We trust the

E♭
B♭
F
Name of Je - sus.
32
CHORUS
B♭
B♭/D
E♭
f
You are the on - ly King for - ev - er.
Al-might-y God, we lift
35
You high - er.
B♭/F
You are the on - ly King for - ev - er.
38
E♭
B♭
For - ev - er-more
You are vic - to - ri - ous.
You are the on - ly King
41
B♭/D
E♭
for - ev - er.
Al-might-y God, we lift
You high - er.
44

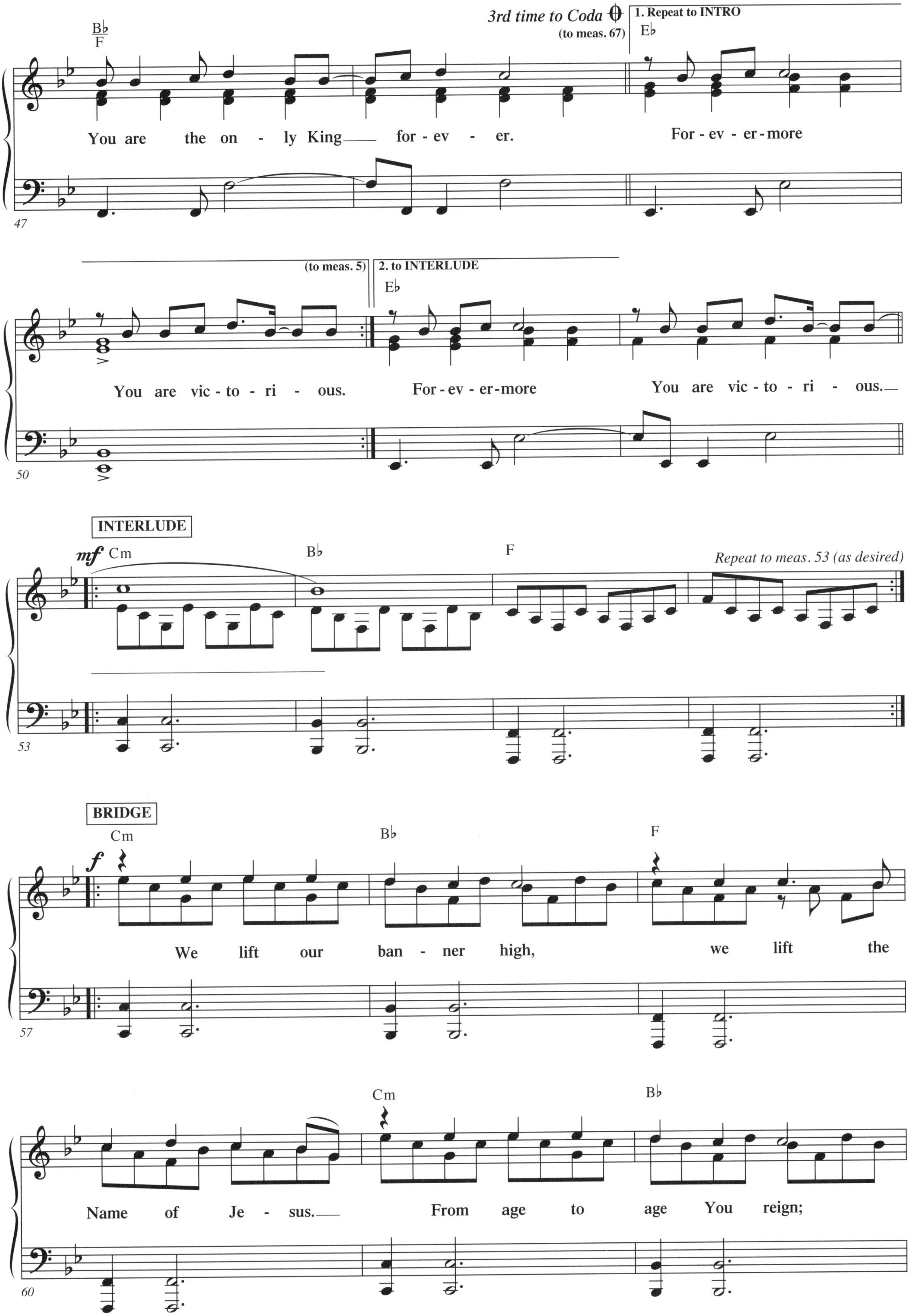
3rd time to Coda
(to meas. 67)
1. Repeat to INTRO
B♭/F
E♭
You are the on - ly King for - ev - er.
For - ev - er - more
(to meas. 5)
2. to INTERLUDE
E♭
You are vic - to - ri - ous.
For - ev - er - more
You are vic - to - ri - ous.
INTERLUDE
mf
Cm
B♭
F
Repeat to meas. 53 (as desired)
BRIDGE
f
Cm
B♭
F
We lift our ban - ner high,
we lift the
Name of Je - sus.
Cm
B♭
From age to age You reign;

1. Repeat BRIDGE
(to meas. 57)
2. to CHORUS
D.S. al Coda
(to meas. 35)
F
Your King - dom has no end.
Your King - dom has no end.
63
CODA
ENDING
E♭
B♭
For - ev - er - more You are vic - to - ri - ous!
67
B♭sus
B♭
70
B♭/D
B♭sus
B♭
73

Chords Used:

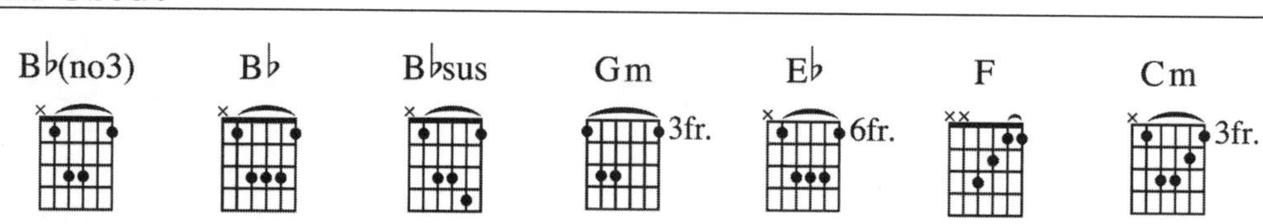
B♭(no3)
B♭
B♭sus
Gm
3fr.
E♭
6fr.
F
Cm
3fr.

Open My Eyes

Words and Music by
BRADEN LANG and REUBEN MORGAN

C
G
D
I see Your fame in all of the earth, and I
I hear Your praise in all of the earth, and I
I know Your love is all that I need, and I
13
Em
C
G
seek to know the ways of Your
seek to know the ways of Your
seek to know the ways of Your
16
1. Repeat to VERSE 2
(to meas. 5)
2., 3. to CHORUS
D
D
heart.
2. Through the seas
heart.
heart.
19
CHORUS
G
f
So o - pen my eyes, O God. O - pen my
22
Em
C2
heart to see all the won - der and the pow -
25

G
- er of Your Name.
By Your
G
Em
grace I'll live.
By Your grace I'll see,
C2
for my life and my sal - va - tion is in You.
1. Repeat to VERSE 3
(to meas. 5)
2. to INSTRUMENTAL
G
mf
3. For You take
INSTRUMENTAL
C
G
D
Em
(Repeat to meas. 41)

BRIDGE
C2 G D
mp–mf
I know Your love is all that I need, and I
1st x: play whole notes
2nd x: as written
45
Em C2 G
seek to know the ways of Your
48
1. Repeat BRIDGE (to meas. 45)
2. to CHORUS
D D
f
heart. heart. So o-pen my
51
CHORUS
G Em
eyes, O God. O - pen my heart to see
55
C2
all the won - der and the pow - er of Your Name.
58

G
G
By Your grace I'll live.
61
Em
By Your grace I'll see, for my life
64
1. Repeat CHORUS (opt.)
C2
G
and my sal - va - tion is in You.
67
(to meas. 55)
2. SONG ENDING
G
So o-pen my
70

Chords Used:

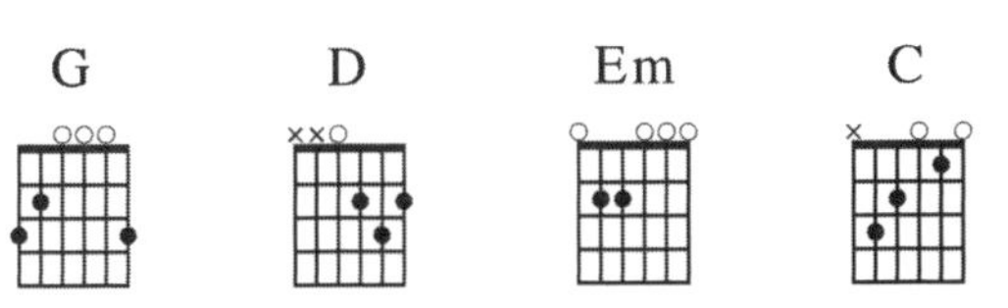
G
D
Em
C

Open Up the Heavens

Words and Music by
MEREDITH ANDREWS, ANDI ROZIER,
JAMES McDONALD, JASON INGRAM,
and STUART GARRARD

Modern acoustic vibe (♩ = 100)

* *Optional vocal intro, which appears here as cue notes, should be sung 1 octave lower.*

PRE-CHORUS
Gm7(4)
Eb2
Gm7(4)
You're the rea - son we're here.
You're the rea - son we're sing - ing.
Eb2
CHORUS
Bb
f
O - pen up the heav - ens, we want to see You.
Eb2
Gm7
O - pen up the flood - gates, a might - y riv - er flow - ing from Your heart,
F
1. Repeat to VERSE 2
Bb
fill - ing ev - 'ry part of our praise.
(to meas. 5)
2. Repeat CHORUS
(to meas. 17)
Eb2
Bb
2. Your
13
16
19
22
25

3. to BRIDGE
B♭
BRIDGE
mf
Show us,
29
show us Your glo - ry.
E♭2
Show us,
show us Your pow - er.
32
Gm7
Show us,
F
show us Your glo - ry, Lord.
1. Repeat BRIDGE
E♭2
35
(to meas. 31)
2. to CHORUS
E♭2
38
B♭
f
E♭2
41

CHORUS
B♭
E♭2
O - pen up the heav - ens, we want to see You. O - pen up the flood - gates,
Gm7
a might - y riv - er flow - ing from Your heart,
F
1. Repeat CHORUS
(to meas. 45)
B♭/E♭
fill - ing ev - 'ry part of our praise.
2. SONG ENDING
B♭

Chords Used:

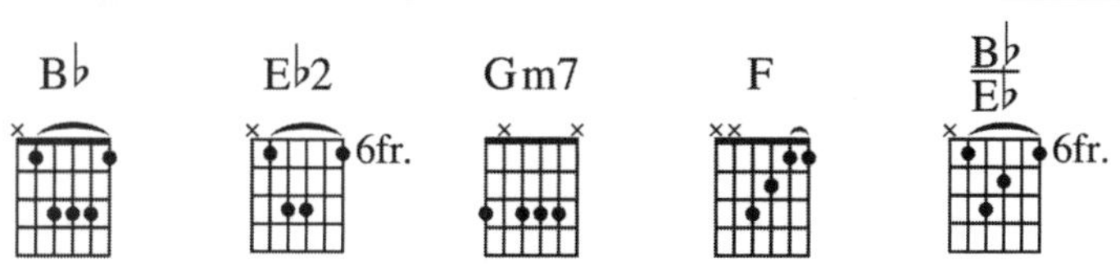
B♭
E♭2
6fr.
Gm7
F
B♭/E♭
6fr.

365 Overwhelmed

Words and Music by
MICHAEL WEAVER and PHIL WICKHAM

VERSE 2, 3
C
G
2. I hear the sound of Your voice. All at
3. I know the pow'r of Your cross. For-
13
D
Em
D
C
once it's a gen - tle and thun - der - ing noise, O God. All that You
giv - en and free; for - ev - er You'll be my God. All that You've
16
G
D
f
are is so o - ver - whelm - ing. I de -
done is so o - ver - whelm - ing.
19
CHORUS
G
D
Em
light my - self in You, cap - ti - vat - ed by Your beau -
(2nd /3rd times) in the glo - ry of Your pres -
22
C
G
D
- ty. I'm o - ver - whelmed, I'm o - ver - whelmed by
- ence.
25

Em C G
You. God, I run in - to Your
D Em C
arms, un - a - shamed be-cause of mer - cy. I'm o - ver - whelmed,
3rd time to Coda (to meas. 55)
1. Repeat to VERSE 3
G D G
mf
I'm o - ver - whelmed by You.
Am7 Em7
(to meas. 14)
2. to BRIDGE
G D/G Em C/E
You.

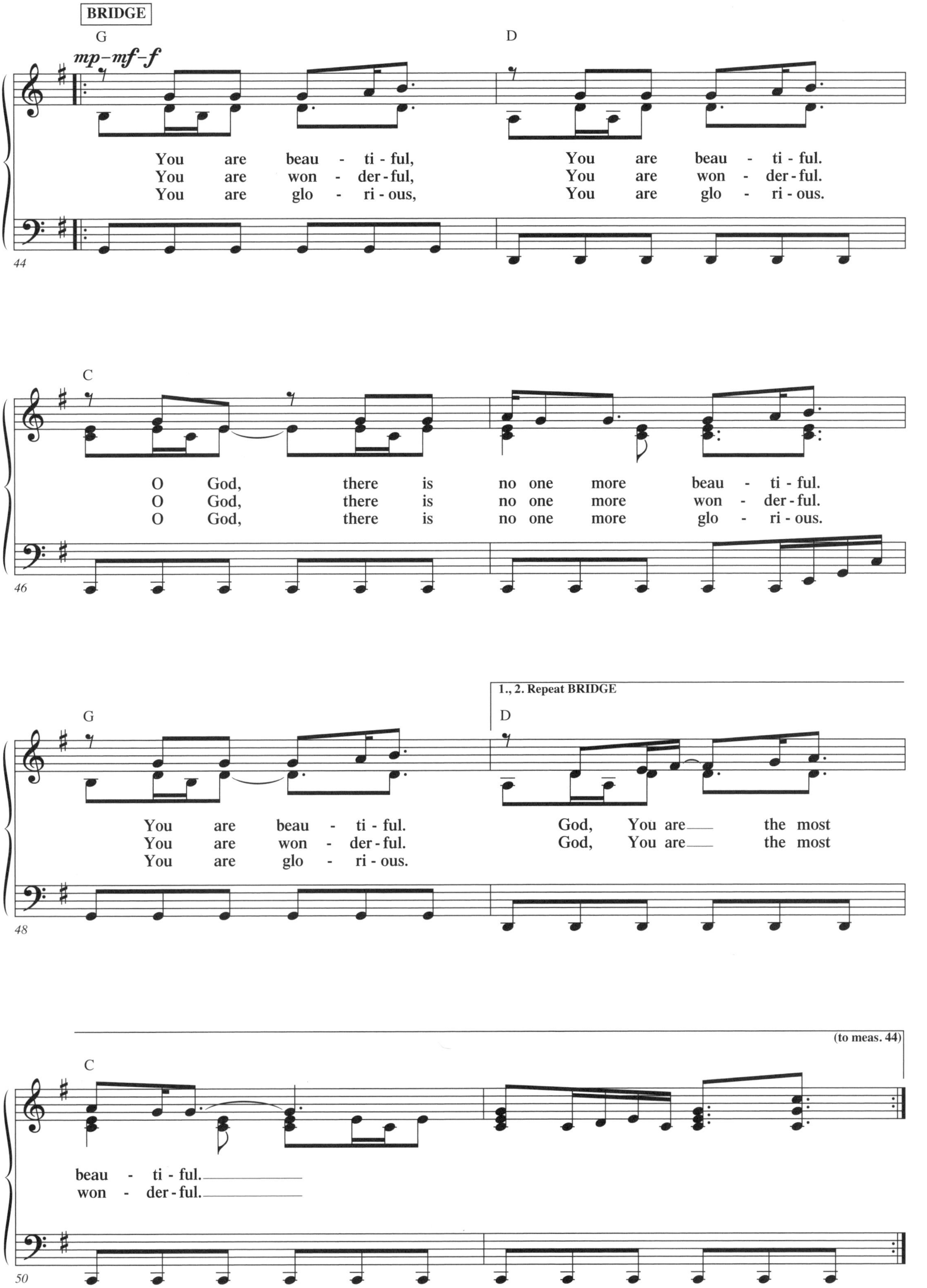
BRIDGE
G
mp–mf–f
D
You are beau - ti - ful, You are beau - ti - ful.
You are won - der - ful, You are won - der - ful.
You are glo - ri - ous, You are glo - ri - ous.
44
C
O God, there is no one more beau - ti - ful.
O God, there is no one more won - der - ful.
O God, there is no one more glo - ri - ous.
46
1., 2. Repeat BRIDGE
G
D
You are beau - ti - ful. God, You are the most
You are won - der - ful. God, You are the most
You are glo - ri - ous.
48
(to meas. 44)
C
beau - ti - ful.
won - der - ful.
50

3. to CHORUS
D/F♯
D
C
D.S. al Coda
(to meas. 22)
God, You are the most glo - ri-ous! I de -
52
CODA
Em
C
G
You. I'm o - ver-whelmed, I'm o - ver -
55
ENDING
D
G
(1st x only)
Am7
whelmed by You.
58
Em
1. Repeat ENDING
(to meas. 59)
C
2. SONG ENDING
C
G
61

Chords Used:

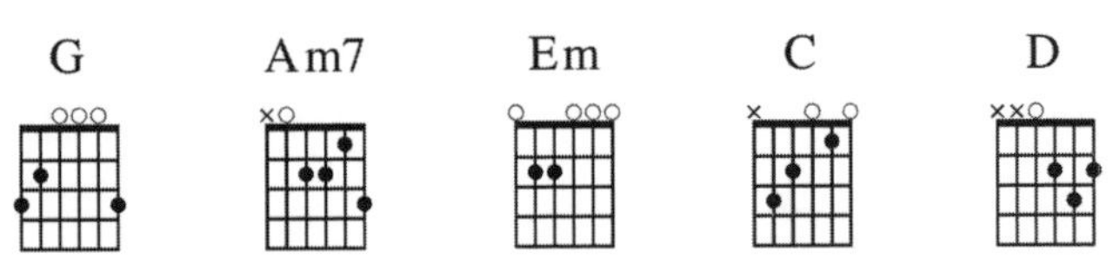
G
Am7
Em
C
D

Remembrance (The Communion Song)

366

Words and Music by
MATT MAHER and MATT REDMAN

PRE-CHORUS
Em7 D/F♯ G2 A
By Your mer - cy we come to Your ta - ble. By Your grace
13
Em7 D/F♯ G2
You are mak - ing us faith - ful.
CHORUS
D Bm7
Lord, we re - mem - ber You,
16
A G2 D A
and re - mem - brance leads us to wor - ship. And as we
19
G2 D A G2 D
wor - ship You, our wor - ship leads to com - mun -
22
3rd time to Coda
(to meas. 46)
A Em7 D/F♯ G2 A
- ion. We re - spond to Your in - vi - ta - tion. We re - mem - ber
25

1. Repeat to VERSE 2
D
G2/D
You.
Em7
(to meas. 6)
2. to BRIDGE
D
f
2. See His You. Dy-ing, You de-
BRIDGE
G A D G A
stroyed our death. Ris-ing, You re-stored our life.
Bm7 A
Lord Je-sus, come in glo-ry. Lord Je-sus, come in
G D A
glo-ry. Lord Je-sus, come in glo-ry.

D.S. al Coda
(to meas. 18)
G
Lord Je - sus, come in glo - ry. Lord, we re -
43
CODA
G2
Em7
D/F♯
- tion. We re-spond to Your in - vi - ta -
46
ENDING
G2
Bm7
A
mf
D
- tion. We re-mem - ber You.
48
G2/D
Em9
(Repeat to m. 48 as desired)
D
51

Chords Used:

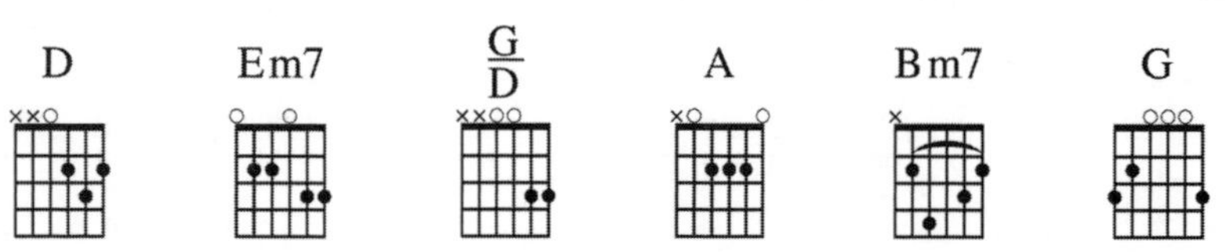
D
Em7
G/D
A
Bm7
G

Scandal of Grace

Words and Music by
JOEL HOUSTON and MATT CROCKER

PRE-CHORUS
A C♯m D
mp–mf
blood. Too much to make sense of it
sing. The day and its trou - bles shall
10
A C♯m D
all, I know that Your love breaks my
come, I know that Your strength is e -
12
A E
fall. The scan - dal of grace, You
nough. The scan - dal of grace, You
14
F♯m D
died in my place so my soul will live. Oh, to be
died in my place so my soul will live.
16
CHORUS
A E
mf–f
like You, give all I have just to know You;
2nd x: play cue notes
19

Dmaj7
Je - sus, there's no one be - side You, for - ev - er the hope in my
1. Repeat to VERSE 2 (to meas. 3)
2. Repeat CHORUS (to meas. 19)
A D F♯m D
heart.
A
heart. Oh, to be
3. to BRIDGE
A D F♯m D A D
heart.
BRIDGE
F♯m D A
And it's all be - cause of You, Je - sus. It's
E F♯m
all be - cause of You, Je - sus. It's all be-

D2
cause of Your love that my soul will live. Oh, to be
38
CHORUS
A
ff–mp
E
like You, give all I have just to know You;
41
Dmaj7
Je - sus, there's no one be - side You, for - ev - er the hope in my
44
1. Repeat CHORUS
(to meas. 41)
2. SONG ENDING
A2
mp
A
heart. Oh, to be heart.
47

Chords Used:

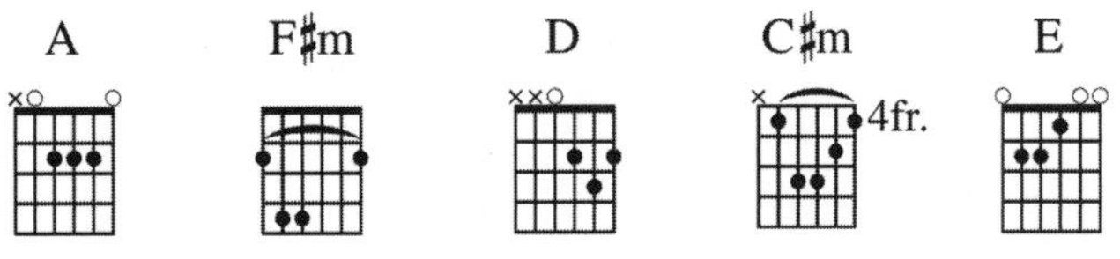

A
F♯m
D
C♯m
4fr.
E

Set a Fire

Words and Music by
WILL REAGAN

Bb/D
Eb
(Repeat to meas. 5)
I want more of You, God. I want more of You, God.
11
CHORUS 2
Bb
Eb
mf
Set a fire down in my soul that I can't con-tain and I can't con-trol.
13
Gm
Eb
I want more of You, God. I want more of You, God.
15
Bb
Eb
Set a fire down in my soul that I can't con-tain and I can't con-trol.
17
Gm
Eb
(Repeat to meas. 13)
I want more of You, God. I want more of You, God.
19

CHORUS 3
f–ff
B♭
E♭
Set a fire down in my soul that I can't con-tain and I can't con-trol.
21
Gm
E♭
I want more of You, God. I want more of You, God.
23
B♭
E♭
Set a fire down in my soul that I can't con-tain and I can't con-trol.
25
(Repeat to meas. 21)
Play 3 times total
Gm
E♭
I want more of You, God. I want more of You, God.
27
CHORUS 4
mp
B♭
E♭
Set a fire down in my soul that I can't con-tain and I can't con-trol.
29

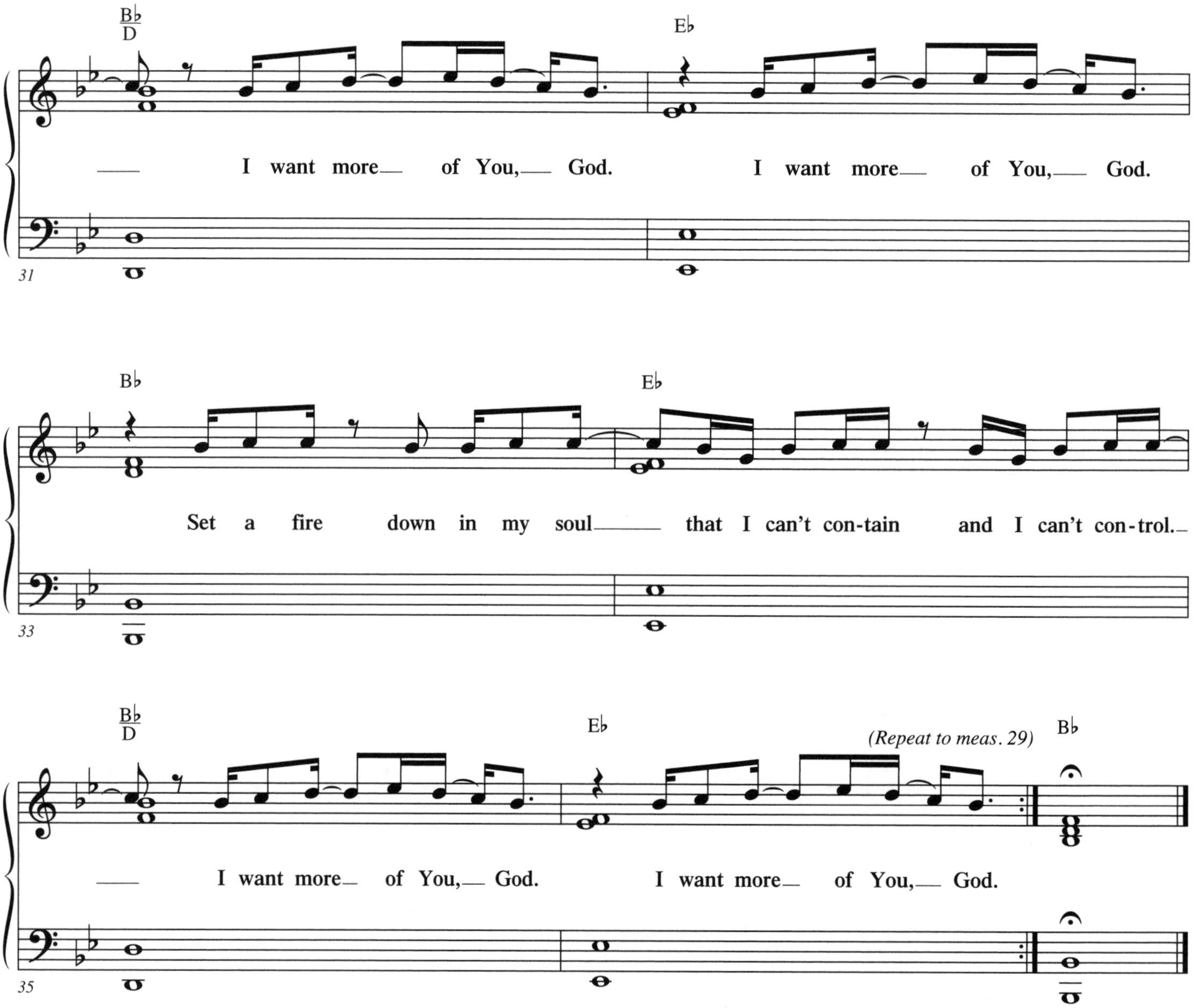
B♭/D
E♭
I want more of You, God. I want more of You, God.
31
B♭
E♭
Set a fire down in my soul that I can't con-tain and I can't con-trol.
33
B♭/D
E♭
(Repeat to meas. 29)
B♭
I want more of You, God. I want more of You, God.
35

Chords Used:

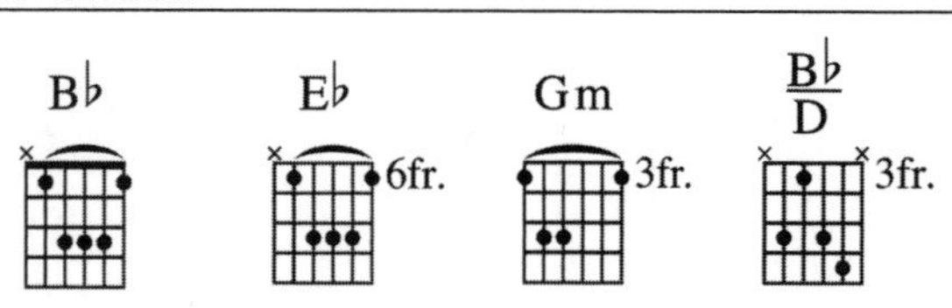
B♭
E♭
6fr.
Gm
3fr.
B♭/D
3fr.

Strong God

369

Words and Music by
MEREDITH ANDREWS, JASON INGRAM,
and JON EGAN

Quiet groove (♩ = 128)
F♯m D A E
mp
VERSE 1, 2
mf
1. Fa - ther to the fa - ther - less, De - fend - er of the weak, Free - dom for the pris - on - er; we sing.
(2.) with us in the wil - der - ness, faith - ful to pro - vide; ev - 'ry breath and ev - 'ry step we see,

PRE-CHORUS
F♯m
D
A
(keyboard written above vocal melody)
This is God in His ho - ly place.
13
C♯m
F♯m
D
This is God, clothed in love and
16
A
(keyboard written above vocal melody)
strength.
19
CHORUS
A
mf–f
E
Sing out. (1st time) Lift your voice and cry out,
Raise your hands and shout out,
21
F♯m
"Awe - some is our strong God. Might - y is our
24

1. Repeat to VERSE 2
(to meas. 5)
2. Repeat CHORUS
D
God!"
2. You're
God!"
27
(to meas. 21)
3. to BRIDGE
D
God!"
30
BRIDGE
Bm
F♯m
A2(no3)
mf–f
There is none high - er, no.
There is none
33
E2
Bm
F♯m
great - er, no.
There is none strong - er than our
36
1., 2. Repeat BRIDGE
(to meas. 33)
3. to CHORUS
Esus
(cresc. 2nd time)
E
Esus
God.
God.
39

CHORUS
E
ff A
Sing out. (1st time) Lift your voice and
Raise your hands and
42
E
F♯m
cry out, "Awe - some is our strong God.
shout out,
45
1. Repeat CHORUS
(to meas. 43)
D
Might - y is our God!"
48
2. SONG ENDING
D
A
God!"
51

Chords Used:

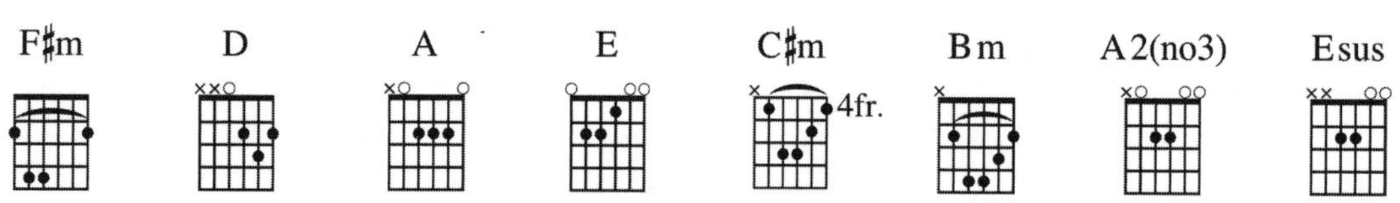
F♯m
D
A
E
C♯m
4fr.
Bm
A2(no3)
Esus

The Only Name
(Yours Will Be)

Words and Music by
BENJI COWART

* *Piano intro may be optionally played 8va.*

2., 3. to PRE-CHORUS
PRE-CHORUS
A
D2
And Yours is the Name, the Name
Esus
A
F♯m7
that saved me; mer - cy and grace, the pow'r that for-gave me. And Your
Dmaj7
E
1. Repeat to VERSE 1
A
love is all I've ev - er need - ed.
(to meas. 5)
2. to CHORUS
(opt. 8va on repeat)
A
f
(1.) Yours will be - ed.
When
CHORUS
A
D2(no3)
I wake up in the Land of Glo - ry with the saints, I will

Bm7
E/G♯
tell my sto - ry. There will be one Name that I pro - claim.
28
1. Repeat CHORUS
(to meas. 25)
2. to INTERLUDE
A
A
When
31
INTERLUDE
ff
A
La la, la la, la la, la la, la la.
34
D2(no3)
Bm7
La la, la la, la la, la la, la la. La la, la la, la la,
37
E/G♯
A
la la, la la la la.
40

BRIDGE
A
D2(no3)
mp–mf
Je - sus,
Je - sus,
43
Bm7
E
G♯
Je - sus,
just that Name.
46
1. Repeat BRIDGE
(to meas. 43)
2. to CHORUS
A
ff
When
49
CHORUS
A
D2(no3)
ff
I wake up in the Land of Glo - ry with the saints, I will
53
Bm7
E
G♯
tell my sto - ry. There will be one Name that I pro - claim.
56

1. Repeat CHORUS
(to meas. 53)
2. to INTERLUDE
A
When
59
INTERLUDE
f
La la, la la, la la, la la, la la.
62
D2(no3)
Bm7
La la, la la, la la, la la, la la.
La la, la la, la la,
65
1. Repeat INTERLUDE
(to meas. 63)
E/G♯
la la, la la la la.
68
2. Repeat INTERLUDE
(to meas. 63)
3. SONG ENDING
poco rit.
la la, la la la la.
la la, la la la la.
71

Chords Used:

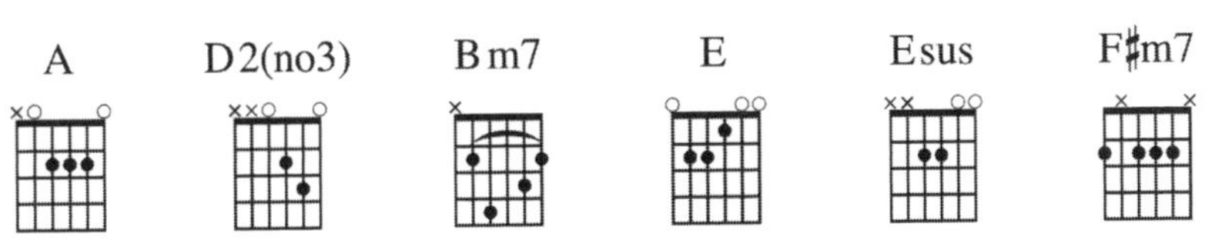
A
D2(no3)
Bm7
E
Esus
F♯m7

371 The Same Love

Words and Music by
MICHAEL ROSSBACK and PAUL BALOCHE

Light pop rock feel (♩ = 102)

A5
D2(no3)
A5
mp
D2(no3)
VERSE 1
mf
A5
D2(no3)
1. You choose the hum - ble and raise them high.
A5
D2(no3)
F♯m7
You choose the weak and make them strong. You heal our bro -
C♯m/E
D2(no3)
- ken-ness in - side and give us life.

CHORUS
A
E
The same love that set the cap - tives free,
(On repeats) The same God that spread the heav - ens wide,
13
F♯m7
D2(no3)
the same love that o - pened eyes to see is call -
the same God that was cru - ci - fied is call -
15
4th time to Coda
(to meas. 32)
1., 3. Repeat CHORUS
F♯m7
- ing us all by name; You are call - ing us all by name.
- ing us all by name; You are call -
17
(to meas. 13)
2. to VERSE 2
D2(no3)
F♯m7
D2(no3)
- ing us all by name.
20
VERSE 2
A5
D2(no3)
mf
2. You take the faith - less one a - side
23

A5
D2(no3)
F♯m7
and speak the words, "You are mine." You call the cyn-
C♯m/E
D2(no3)
D.S. al Coda
(to meas. 13)
-ic and the proud; "Come to Me now."
CODA
F♯m7
D2(no3)
INTERLUDE
ff
E
F♯m7 D2(no3)
-ing us all by name. Oh, oh,
E
F♯m7 D2(no3)
1. Repeat INTERLUDE
(to meas. 34)
oh, oh. Oh,
2. to BRIDGE
BRIDGE
mp–f
A
You're call - ing,

1, 2, 3. Repeat BRIDGE
(to meas. 40)
E
F♯m7
D2(no3)
You're call - ing, You're call - ing us to the cross.
41
4. to CHORUS
D2(no3)
CHORUS
f
A
to the cross.
The same love that set the
(2nd time) The same God that spread the
44
E
F♯m7
cap - tives free, the same love that o - pened
heav - ens wide, the same God that was
46
D2(no3)
A
eyes to see is call - ing us all by name;
cru - ci - fied is call - ing us all by name;
48
1. Repeat CHORUS
(to meas. 45)
E
F♯m7
D2(no3)
You are call - ing us all by name.
You are call -
50

2. to INTERLUDE
F♯m7
D2(no3)
INTERLUDE
ff
E
F♯m7 D2(no3)
- ing us all by name. Oh, oh,
53
E
F♯m7 D2(no3)
1. Repeat INTERLUDE
(to meas. 55)
oh, oh. Oh,
56
2. to SONG ENDING
ENDING
mp
A
E
You're call - ing, You're call - ing,
59
F♯m7
1. Repeat ENDING
(to meas. 61)
D2(no3)
2. SONG ENDING
D2(no3)
You're call - ing us to the cross. to the cross.
63

Chords Used:

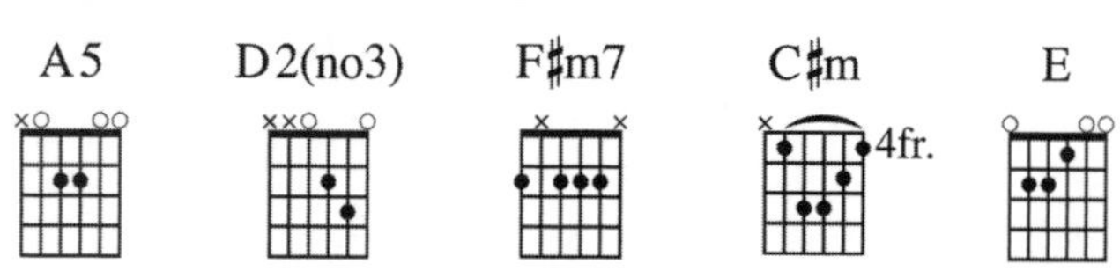
A5
D2(no3)
F♯m7
C♯m
4fr.
E

This I Believe
(The Creed)

372

Words and Music by
BEN FIELDING and MATT CROCKER

CHORUS
mf
F Gm B♭ C
I be-lieve in God our Fa - ther, I be-lieve in Christ the Son,
13
Dm B♭
I be-lieve in the Ho - ly Spir - it; our God is Three in One.
15
F Gm B♭ C
I be-lieve in the res - ur - rec - tion, that we will rise a - gain,
17
Dm
1. Repeat to VERSE 2
B♭ C B♭ Dm
8va
for I be-lieve in the Name of Je - sus.
19
C F/A B♭ Dm C F/A
(8va)
(to meas. 5)
22

2. to BRIDGE
BRIDGE
B♭ C F B♭ Dm
f
Name of Je - sus. I be - lieve in You.
C F/A B♭ Dm C F/A
I be - lieve You rose a - gain. I be-
1. Repeat BRIDGE
(to meas. 27)
B♭ C F F/A
- lieve that Je - sus Christ is Lord. And I be -
2. to CHORUS
CHORUS
F F Gm
mp–mf–f
1. I be-lieve in life e - ter - nal.
2., 3. I be-lieve in God our Fa - ther,
B♭ C Dm
I be-lieve in the Vir - gin birth. I be-lieve in the saints' com - mun - ion
I be-lieve in Christ the Son, I be-lieve in the Ho - ly Spir - it;

B♭ F Gm
and in Your ho - ly Church. I be-lieve in the res - ur - rec - tion,
our God is Three in One. I be-lieve in the res - ur - rec - tion,
40
B♭ C Dm
when Je - sus comes a - gain, for I be - lieve in the
that we will rise a - gain, for I be - lieve in the
42
1. Repeat CHORUS
(to meas. 37)
B♭ C F
Name of Je - sus.
44
2. Repeat CHORUS
(to meas. 37)
3. SONG ENDING
B♭ C B♭ C
Name of Je - sus. Name of Je - sus.
47
Dm B♭ C F
For I be - lieve in the Name of Je - sus.
49

Chords Used:

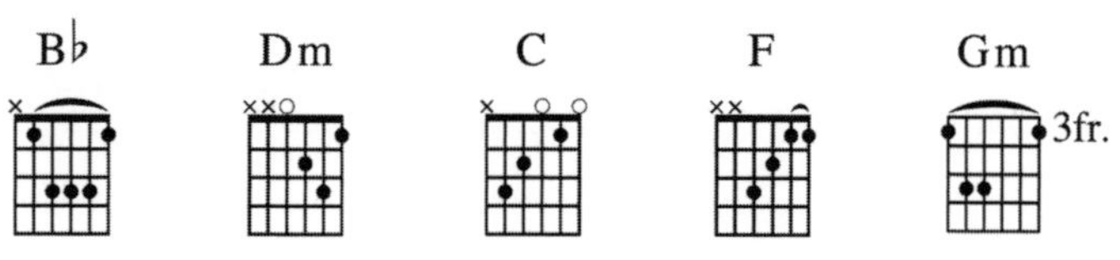
B♭
Dm
C
F
Gm
3fr.

This Is Amazing Grace

373

Words and Music by
JEREMY RIDDLE, JOSH FARRO, and PHIL WICKHAM

Driving pop rock (♩ = 98)
G
G/C
f
VERSE 1, 2
mf
G
1. Who breaks the pow - er of sin and dark - ness?
2. Who shakes the whole earth with ho - ly thun - der,
G/C
(2nd time sing cue note)
Whose love is might - y and so much strong - er?
and leaves us breath - less in awe and won - der?
Em7
D
The King of Glo - ry, the King a - bove all kings.
The King of Glo - ry, the King a - bove all kings.
4
7
9

1. Repeat to VERSE 2
(to meas. 5)
2. to CHORUS
G/C
G/C
11
CHORUS
G
f
This is a - maz - ing grace,
this is un - fail - ing love,
14
8vb
G/C
Em7
that You would take my place,
17
D
that You would bear my cross.
You laid down Your life
20
G
G/C
that I would be set free.
23

Em7
D
Whoa, Je - sus, I sing for all that You've done for me.
G
G/C
VERSE 3, 4
mf
3. Who brings our cha - os back in - to or - der?
4. Who rules the na - tions with truth and jus - tice,
Who makes the or - phan a son and daugh - ter?
shines like the sun in all of its bril - liance?
1. Repeat to VERSE 4
(to meas. 33)
The King of Glo - ry, the King of Glo - ry.
26
29
33
35
37

2. to CHORUS
Em7
D
G/C
The King of Glo - ry, the King a - bove all kings. Yeah,
CHORUS
G
f
this is a - maz - ing grace, this is un - fail - ing love,
8vb
G/C
Em7
that You would take my place,
D
that You would bear my cross. You laid down Your life,
G
G/C
that I would be set free.

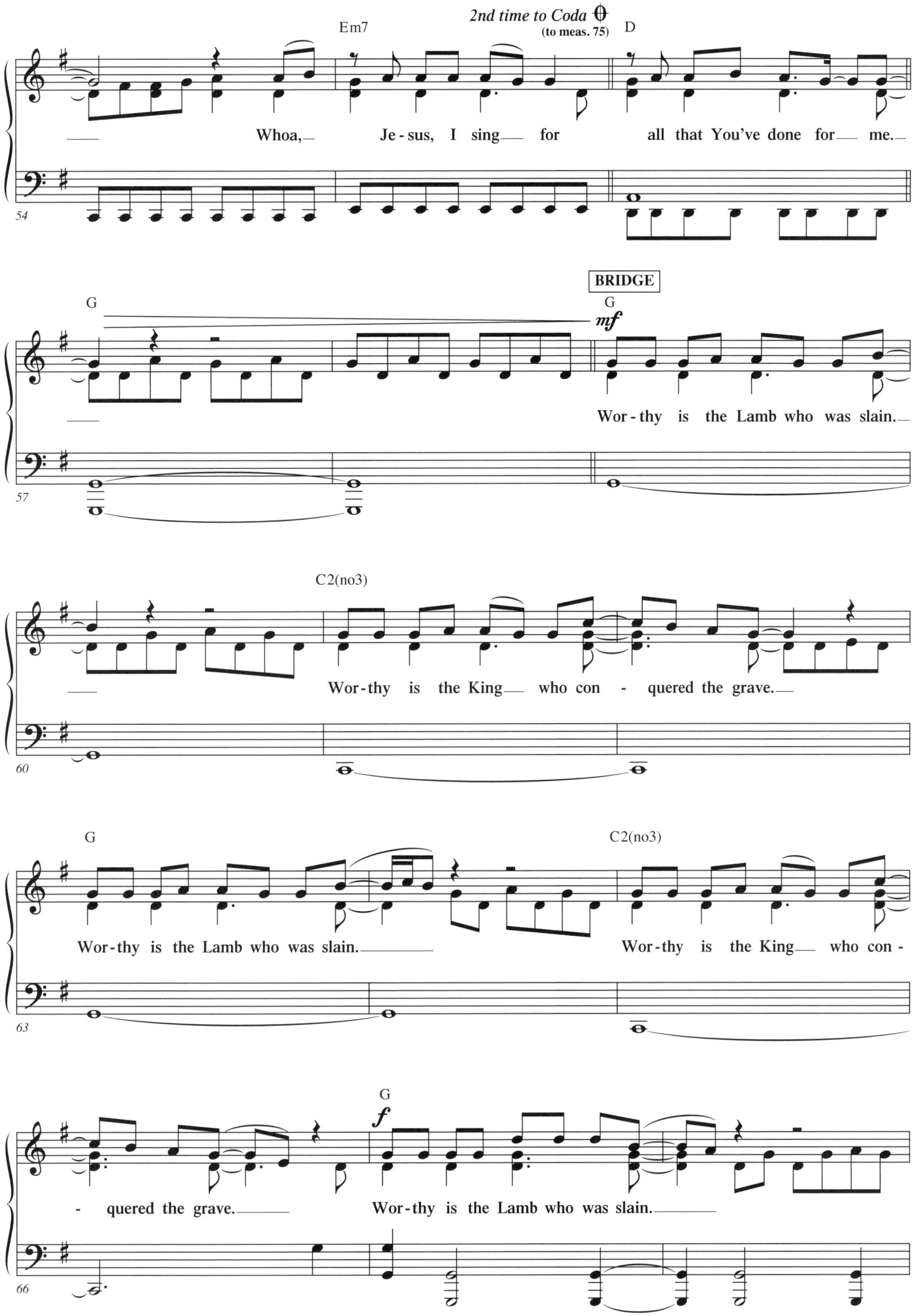
2nd time to Coda
(to meas. 75)
Em7
D
Whoa, Je - sus, I sing for all that You've done for me.
G
BRIDGE
G
mf
Wor - thy is the Lamb who was slain.
C2(no3)
Wor - thy is the King who con - quered the grave.
G
C2(no3)
Wor - thy is the Lamb who was slain.
Wor - thy is the King who con - quered the grave.
G
f
Wor - thy is the Lamb who was slain.
54
57
60
63
66

C2(no3)
Em
Wor-thy is the King who con - quered the grave.
Wor-thy is the Lamb who was slain,
69
G
G/C
D.S. al Coda
(to meas. 43)
wor - thy, wor - thy, wor - thy!
This is a-maz-ing grace,
72
CODA
D
ENDING
ff
G
all that You've done for me.
75
G/C
(Repeat as desired to meas. 76)
G
77

Chords Used:

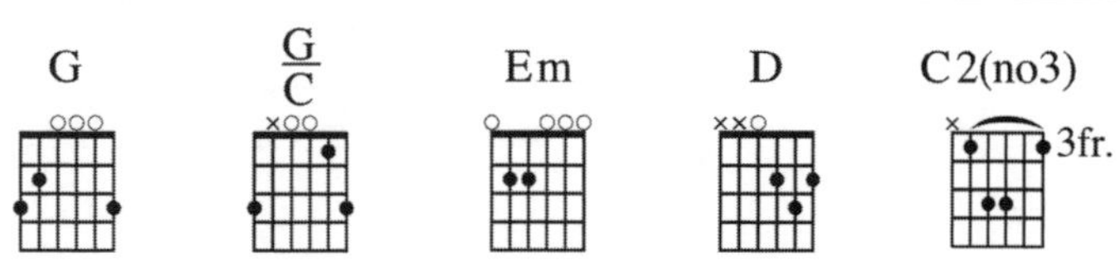
G
G/C
Em
D
C2(no3)
3fr.

Thrive

374

Words and Music by
MARK HALL and MATTHEW WEST

Acoustic folk rock (♩ = 115)
E
mf
INTRO
A
E
A
E
f
Oh!
A
E
Bsus
Oh!
VERSE 1, 2
A2
mf
1. Here in this worn and wea-ry land where man-y a dream has
2. In - to Your Word we're dig-gin' deep to know our Fa - ther's

E
A2
died,
heart.
like a tree plant - ed by the wa -
In - to the world we're reach - ing out
E
- ter, we nev - er will run dry.
to show them Who You are.
PRE-CHORUS
C♯m7
E
So, Liv - ing Wa - ter flow - ing through, God, we
C♯m7
E
C♯m7
thirst for more of You. Fill our hearts and flood our
E
Bsus
souls with one de - sire: Just to

CHORUS
A2
f–f–mp
E
A2
know You and to make You known, we lift Your Name on
29
E
A2
E
high. Shine like the sun, make dark - ness run and
32
Bsus
(3rd x)
A2
f
hide. We know we were made for
35
E
C♯m7
Bsus
so much more than or - di - nar - y lives. It's
38
A2
E
Bsus
3rd time to Coda
(to meas. 61)
time for us to more than just sur - vive;
41

1. Repeat to INTRO
(to meas. 5)
2. to BRIDGE
A2 Bsus E A2 Bsus
we were made to thrive.
we were made to
44
E
thrive.
47
BRIDGE
E A2 B(4)
mf
(Repeat to meas. 51)
Joy un-speak-a-ble, faith un-sink-a-ble, love un-stop-pa-ble, an-y-thing is pos-si-ble.
51
E A2
Joy un-speak-a-ble, faith un-sink-a-ble, love un-stop-pa-ble,
55
1. Repeat
(to meas. 55)
2. to CHORUS
D.S. al Coda
(to meas. 29)
B(4) B(4)
an-y-thing is pos-si-ble. an-y-thing is pos-si-ble! Just to
58

CODA
ENDING
A2 Bsus E A E
we were made to thrive. Oh!
A E A E
Oh!
Bsus
1. Repeat ENDING (to meas. 63)
2. SONG ENDING
A2 Bsus E
We were made to thrive.
E(no3)

Chords Used:

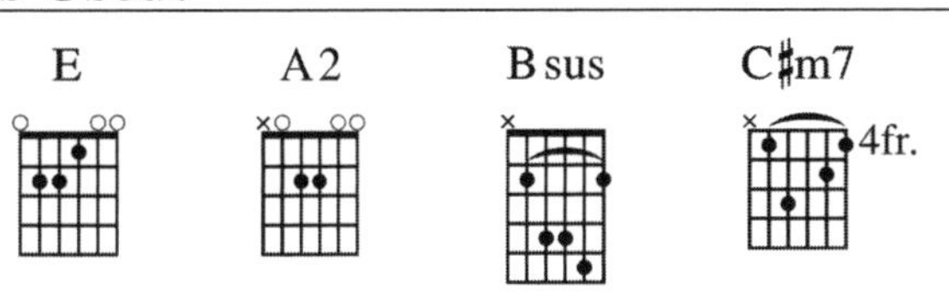
E
A2
Bsus
C♯m7
4fr.

Victor's Crown

Words and Music by
DARLENE ZSCHECH, ISRAEL HOUGHTON,
and KARI JOBE

Am7
G/B
C
Help and my De - fend - er, You're my Sav - ior and my Friend. By Your
glo - ry fill this tem - ple, let Your pow - er o - ver - flow.
Je - sus, the Mes - si - ah; You're the Hope of all the world.
10
1. Repeat to VERSE 2 (to meas. 6)
2., 3. to CHORUS
Dm7
F/C
Gsus
G
mf–f
grace I live and breathe to wor - ship You. 2. At the You. Hal - le -
12
CHORUS
F
G
C
lu - jah! You have o - ver - come, You have
15
Dm7
Am7
o - ver - come. Hal - le - lu - jah! Je - sus, You have
18
1. Repeat to VERSE 3
f
o - ver - come the world.
21

(to meas. 6)
2. to INSTRUMENTAL
F C G Dm7 G
mf
3. You are o - ver-come the world.
24
INSTRUMENTAL
mf–f
F C G Dm7 F C G
(Repeat to meas. 27)
27
BRIDGE
mf–f–ff
F C G Dm7
Ev - 'ry high thing must come down, ev - 'ry strong-hold shall be bro - ken.
31
F C
1., 2., 3. Repeat BRIDGE
(to meas. 31)
G
You wear the Vic - tor's crown; You o - ver-come, You o - ver-come.
33
4. to VERSE 4
G F
You o - ver-come, You o - ver-come.
35

VERSE 4
mf
Am7
G/B
4. At the cross the work was fin - ished; You were
C
Dm7
C/E
bur - ied in the ground. But the grave could not con - tain You, for You
F
C
Csus
wear the Vic - tor's crown.
C
Csus
C
Csus
C
ff
Hal - le -
CHORUS
ff
F
G
C
F
C
lu - jah! You have o - ver - come, You have

G
Dm7
F
G
Am7
o - ver-come. Hal - le - lu - jah! Je - sus, You have
51
Dm7
G
BRIDGE
F
C
mf-f-ff
o - ver - come the world. Ev - 'ry high thing must come down,
54
G
Dm7
F
C
ev - 'ry strong-hold shall be bro - ken. You wear the Vic - tor's crown;
56
1. Repeat BRIDGE (as desired)
(to meas. 55)
2. SONG ENDING
G
G
rit.
F
You o - ver-come, You o - ver-come! You o - ver-come, You o - ver-come!
58

Chords Used:

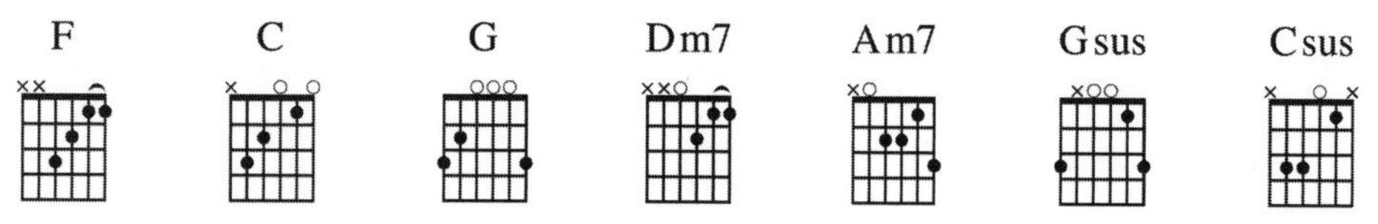
F
C
G
Dm7
Am7
Gsus
Csus

We Believe

376

Words and Music by
MATT HOOPER, RICHIE FIKE,
and TRAVIS RYAN

With anticipation (♩ = 65)

C
F/C
mp
C
F/C
3
VERSE 1
C
F/C
1. In this time of des - per - a - tion,
5
C
F/C
when all we know is doubt and fear,
7
Am7
F
there is on - ly one Foun - da - tion; we be-lieve,
9

C
F/C
we be-lieve.
11
C
mf
F/C
In this bro - ken gen-er-a - tion,
13
C
F/C
when all is dark, You help us see.
15
Am7
F
There is on - ly one sal - va - tion; we be-lieve,
17
C
F/C
f
we be-lieve. We be-lieve
19

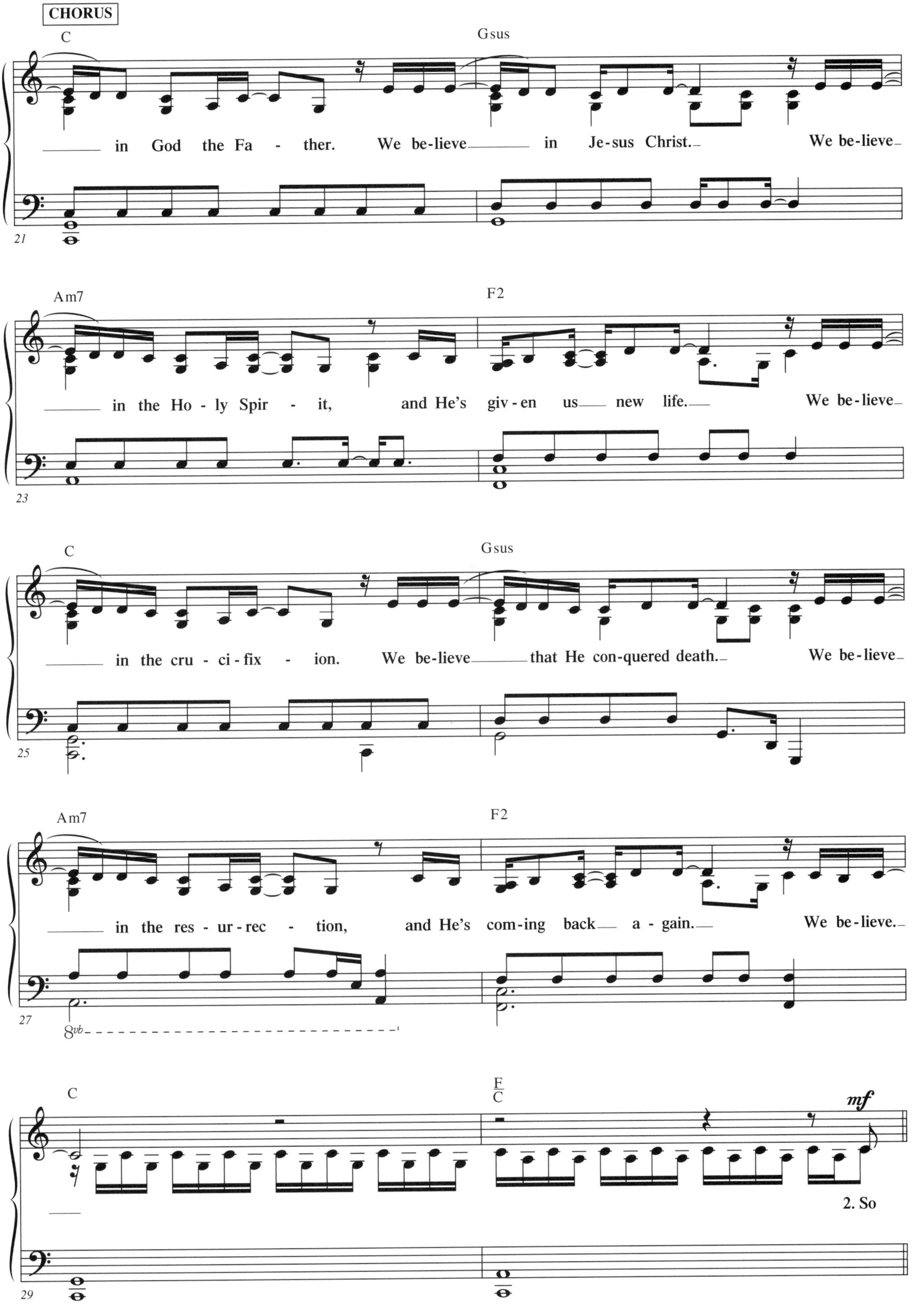
CHORUS
C
Gsus
in God the Fa - ther. We be-lieve in Je-sus Christ. We be-lieve
Am7
F2
in the Ho - ly Spir - it, and He's giv-en us new life. We be-lieve
C
Gsus
in the cru - ci-fix - ion. We be-lieve that He con-quered death. We be-lieve
Am7
F2
in the res - ur-rec - tion, and He's com-ing back a - gain. We be-lieve.
8vb
C
F
C
mf
2. So

VERSE 2
C
F/C
let our faith be more than an - thems,
31
C
F/C
great-er than the songs we sing.
33
Am7
F
And in our weak - ness and temp - ta - tions, we be-lieve,
35
C
F/C
f
we be-lieve! We be-lieve
37
CHORUS
C
Gsus
in God the Fa - ther. We be-lieve in Je-sus Christ. We be-lieve
39

Am7
F2
in the Holy Spirit, and He's given us new life. We believe
41
C
Gsus
in the crucifixion. We believe that He conquered death. We believe
43
Am7
F2
in the resurrection, and He's coming back again. Let the lost
45
BRIDGE
F2
Gsus
Am7
C/E
be found and the dead be raised. In the here and now, let love invade. Let the church
47
F2
Gsus
Am7
C/E
live loud! Our God, we'll say, "We believe! We believe!" And the gates
49

F2 Gsus Am7 C/E
of hell will not pre - vail, for the pow'r of God has torn the veil. Now we know
F2 Gsus Am7 G/B
Your love will nev - er fail. We be-lieve! We be-lieve! We be-lieve
CHORUS
C Gsus
sub. mf
in God the Fa - ther. We be-lieve in Je-sus Christ. We be-lieve
Am7 F2
ff
in the Ho - ly Spir - it, and He's giv-en us new life. We be-lieve
C Gsus
in the cru - ci - fix - ion. We be-lieve that He con-quered death. We be-lieve

Am7
F2
in the res - ur - rec - tion, and He's com - ing back, He's com - ing back a - gain.
61
ENDING
C
Gsus
He's com - ing back a - gain!
63
Am7
F2
We be - lieve!
65
C(no3)
67

Chords Used:

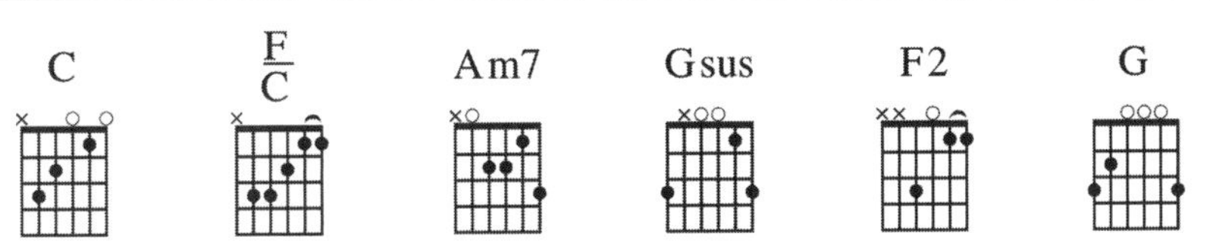
C
F/C
Am7
Gsus
F2
G

377

Whom Shall I Fear
(God of Angel Armies)

Words and Music by
CHRIS TOMLIN, ED CASH,
and SCOTT CASH

Pop rock ballad (♩ = 74)
B♭(no3)
B♭maj7/C
B♭maj7/D
mp
E♭2
VERSE 1
B♭2
1. You hear me when I call.
B♭2/C
B♭2/D
You are my Morn - ing Song.
E♭2
Though dark - ness fills the night,
E♭2/D
F/C
it can - not hide the Light.

Gm7
Eb2
Whom shall I fear?
9
Bb2
Bb2/C
Bb2/D
You crush the en - e - my un - der - neath my feet.
11
Eb2
Eb2/D
F/C
You are my Sword and Shield, though trou - bles lin - ger still.
13
Gm7
Eb2
Whom shall I fear?
15
CHORUS
Gm7
F
Bb
Gm7
F
Bb
mf-f
I know Who goes be - fore me, I know Who stands be - hind:
17

Gm7 E♭2 F B♭ Gm7 F B♭
the God of an - gel ar - mies is al - ways by my side! The One Who reigns for - ev - er,
19
2nd time to Coda
(to meas. 35)
Gm7 F B♭ Gm7 E♭2 F
He is a Friend of mine. The God of an - gel ar - mies is al - ways by my
22
B♭(no3) B♭maj7/C B♭maj7/D
mf
Like intro
(keyboard written above vocal)
side!
25
VERSE 2
B♭
mf
2. My strength is in Your Name, for You a - lone can save.
27
E♭2 E♭2/F
You will de - liv - er me. Yours is the vic - to - ry.
29

Gm7
E♭2
Whom shall I fear?
31
Gm7
E♭2
F(4)
D.S. al Coda
(to meas. 17)
Whom shall I fear?
33
CODA
B♭
f
BRIDGE
E♭2
B♭
side! And noth - ing formed a - gainst me shall
35
F(4)
B♭
E♭2
stand! You hold the whole world in Your hands.
37
B♭
Gm7
F(4)
I'm hold - ing on to Your prom - is - es; You are
40

1. Repeat BRIDGE
(to meas. 36)
2. to CHORUS
Eb2 F(4) Eb2
faith - ful, You are faith - ful.
faith - ful, You are
F(4) Gm7 F/A
faith - ful, You are faith - ful.
CHORUS
mp
Gm7 F Bb Gm7 F Bb Gm7 Eb2
I know Who goes be-fore me, I know Who stands be-hind: the God of an-gel ar-mies
F Bb Gm7 F Bb Gm7 F Bb
is al-ways by my side! The One Who reigns for-ev-er, He is a Friend of mine.
Gm7 Eb2
The God of an - gel ar - mies is al - ways by my side!

B♭2
F(4)
A
Gm7
f
I know Who goes be-fore me,
I know Who stands be-hind:
the God of an-gel ar-mies
56
E♭2
B♭2
is al-ways by my side!
The One Who reigns for-ev-er,
59
F(4)
A
Gm7
E♭2
He is a Friend of mine.
The God of an-gel ar-mies
is al-ways by my side!
61
ENDING
Gm7
E♭2
mp
molto rit.
B♭(no3)
The God of an-gel ar-mies
is al-ways by my side!
64

Chords Used:

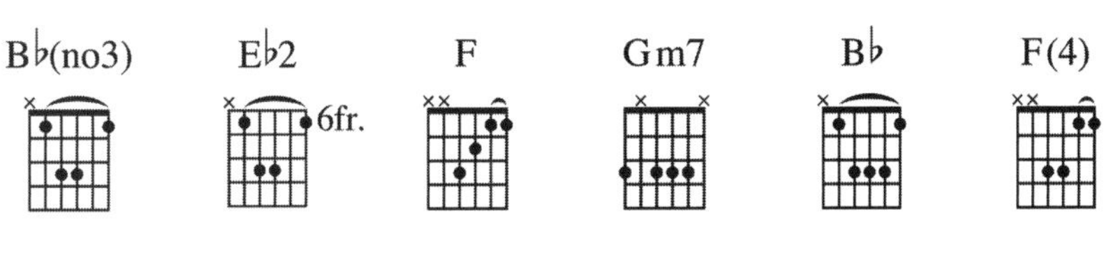
B♭(no3)
E♭2
6fr.
F
Gm7
B♭
F(4)

378 Worship the Great I AM

Words and Music by
WALKER BEACH

Reverent, worshipful (♩ = 68)

C Eb Bb F C Eb
Wor - ship the Great I AM.
Bb F C Eb Bb F
2nd time to Coda
(to meas. 33)
VERSE 2
C(no3) Eb Bb F C(no3) Eb
mf
2. Glo - ry to the Prince of Life, sa - cred Son of
Bb F C(no3) Eb Bb F
God. Ris - en to glo - ry, vowed His re - turn - ing.
C(no3) Eb Bb F
D.S. al Coda
(to meas. 13)
Christ shall come a - gain.

CODA
VERSE 3
C Eb Bb F C(no3) Eb
mf
3. Glo - ry to the
33
Bb F C(no3) Eb Bb F
Prom - ised One, Ho - ly Spir - it of God.
36
C(no3) Eb Bb F
Pour out up - on us pow - er from Heav - en.
39
C(no3) Eb Bb F
Fill us with Your love.
41
CHORUS
C Eb Bb F
ff
Wor - thy, wor - thy, Je - sus is wor - thy.
43

C Eb Bb F C Eb
Praise to the Son of Man. Glo - ry and hon - or
(2nd time) Those who a - dore You,
Bb F
1. Repeat CHORUS (to meas. 43)
C Eb Bb F
crown You for - ev - er. Wor - ship the Great I AM.
bow down be - fore You.
2. to SONG ENDING
C Eb Bb F
ENDING
C(no3)
decresc.
Wor - ship the Great I AM.
Csus C(no3) Csus C(no3)
(opt. W.L. ad libs)
(Repeat to meas. 53)

Chords Used:

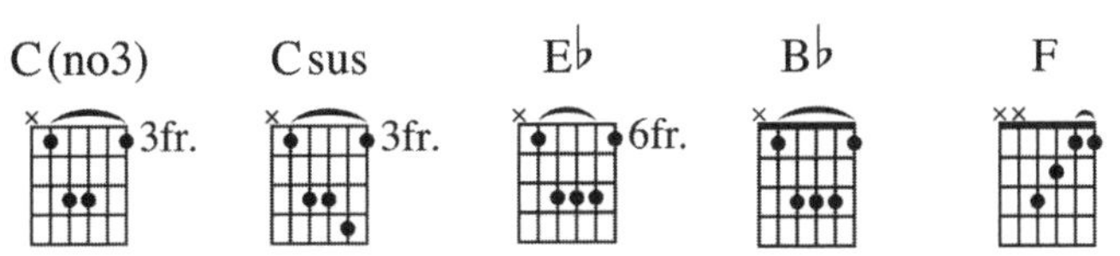
C(no3)
3fr.
Csus
3fr.
Eb
6fr.
Bb
F

379 Your Love Never Fails

Words and Music by
ANTHONY SKINNER and CHRIS McCLARNEY

Dm7
B♭2
F
love nev - er fails.
love nev - er fails.
13
C
Dm7
B♭2
I know I still make mis-takes, but
The chasm is far too wide;
16
F
C
Dm7
You have new mer-cies for me ev-'ry day. Your love nev - er fails.
I nev-er thought I'd reach the oth-er side. Your love nev - er fails.
19
B♭2
F
C
22
CHORUS
B♭
F
C
You stay the same through the a - ges; Your
25

Gm7 Bb F
love nev - er chang - es. There may be pain in the night, but
28
C Gm7
joy comes in the morn - ing.
31
Bb F C
And when the o - ceans rage I don't have
33
3rd time to Coda
(to meas. 62)
Gm7 Bb F
to be a-fraid, be-cause I know that You love me.
36
1. Repeat to VERSE 2
C Bb
Your love nev - er fails.
39

(to meas. 9)
2. to INSTRUMENTAL
Dm7
C
C
INSTRUMENTAL
f
B♭
Dm7
C
1. Repeat INSTRUMENTAL
(to meas. 47)
2. to BRIDGE
You make
BRIDGE
B♭2
mf–mf–f
Dm7
C
all things work to-geth-er for my good.
(3rd x: LH play quarter notes)
B♭2
Dm7
You make all things work to-geth-er for my

1,. 2. Repeat BRIDGE
(to meas. 52)
3. to CHORUS
D.S. al Coda
(to meas. 25)
C
C
— good.
You make—
— good.
CODA
C
Csus
C
Csus
C
ENDING
B♭
ff
Dm7
C
(Repeat to meas. 64)
B♭2

Chords Used:

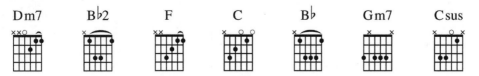

Dm7
B♭2
F
C
B♭
Gm7
Csus